PSYCHOLOGY OF THREAT

PSYCHOLOGY OF EMOTIONS, MOTIVATIONS AND ACTIONS

Additional books in this series can be found on Nova's website under the Series tab.

Additional e-books in this series can be found on Nova's website under the e-book tab.

PSYCHOLOGY OF EMOTIONS, MOTIVATIONS AND ACTIONS

PSYCHOLOGY OF THREAT

BRYAN O. HUNTER
AND
TONY J. ROMERO
EDITORS

nova publishers
New York

For permission to use material from this book please contact us:
Telephone 631-231-7269; Fax 631-231-8175
Web Site: http://www.novapublishers.com

NOTICE TO THE READER

LIBRARY OF CONGRESS CATALOGING-IN-PUBLICATION DATA

Psychology of threat / editors, Bryan O. Hunter and Tony J. Romero.
    p. cm.
Includes index.
ISBN 978-1-62257-344-8 (hbk.)
1. Threat (Psychology) I. Hunter, Bryan O. II. Romero, Tony J.
BF575.T45P79 2012
155.9--dc23
                    2012022827

Published by Nova Science Publishers, Inc. † New York

CONTENTS

PREFACE

In this book, the authors present current research in the psychology of threat. Topics discussed include the processing of threatening health information which promotes disease preventive behaviors; psychological reactions to threats of self-integrity; human reactions to threat from a group-level perspective; stereotype threat; cognitive self-regulation skills; and measuring threat as it relates to social policy.

As explained in Chapter 1, the integrity of the self can be defined as the psychological experience that our actions are sensible and goal directed, that we are in control of them, that our behavior is morally adequate, that we are socially included, that our existence is coherent and continuous. Having self-integrity means dealing with our environment in a way that will lead to positive outcomes.

When self-integrity is threatened we experience a motivation to restore it. Depending on the aspect of integrity that is threatened such motivation is associated with different cognitive, emotional and behavioral responses. These responses can be either defensive or adapting.

Taking a comprehensive perspective to explain how people deal with threats to the self, this chapter subsumes psychological reactions to threats to the self in terms of cognitive dissonance, psychological reactance, self-regulation, self-affirmation, belongingness, fairness, self-esteem and self-continuity.

Threatening health information has the goal to encourage and motivate people to engage in health promoting and disease preventive behaviours and thus reduce health problems and costs in our society. Evidence shows however that threatening health information often fails to bring about a successful behavioural change. Although the frequently used method of health threat information is assumed to lead to more systematic processing of information containing recommended actions, empirical findings have detected defensive responses towards the health threat information itself, especially among those for whom the health threat is high as opposed to low self-relevant. Chapter 2 provides insights in the ways people process (self-relevant) threatening health information by studying attention allocation processes during message exposure. Measuring attention processes for health education messages is crucial because attention for the health message is a prerequisite for effective health education. The authors used measures of EEG, eye movements and reaction times to measure attention processes non-invasively and objectively during message processing. In three empirical studies that will be reported and discussed supported the hypothesis that threatening health information can cause defensive reactions, especially when the information is self-relevant. The integration of neuroscience in health psychology led to a more complete understanding of the underlying attention processes for threatening health information by providing evidence that defensive responses are already present in the very early stages of information processing, at the basic level of attention allocation. It is concluded that communicating self-relevant information and coping information, instead of threatening health information, are promising strategies to increase attention from the reader for the health information.

When God looked upon man, he or she contended that, "It is not good for the man to be alone." (Genesis, 2:18). As humans, we lack the physical strength of true predators, or the speed of those hunted by them; our strength lies in our combined efforts to overcome threat. Research on group-level reactions to threat, however, is scarce. In Chapter 3, the authors will review theory and research on social defense theory (SDT) – a theory that tries to shed light on human reactions to threat from a group-level perspective. SDT suggests that dispositional variables such as attachment orientations may influence people's responses under conditions of threat and related-stress. Some individuals (those scoring relatively high on measures of attachment anxiety) are chronically hypervigilant and alert to potential threats and dangers; they have heightened mental accessibility to what my colleagues and I call sentinel-related schemas, which allow them to detect threats sooner than others and communicate these threats to other members of their group. Other individuals (those scoring relatively high on measures of attachment-related avoidance) are less vigilant to threat than their anxious counterparts; yet, once alerted to a threat, they are likely to take protective action more rapidly and effectively than others. Finally, people scoring relatively low on measures of attachment anxiety and avoidance (i.e., the relatively secure ones) are likely to lead and manage collective efforts to deal with threats, although they are less vigilant to threats than anxious individuals and slower to respond to threats than avoidant individuals. Because each of these personality patterns contributes to effective responses, SDT predicts that groups containing all three kinds of people will be more effective than less heterogeneous groups when dealing with threats and dangers. That is, heterogeneous groups may exhibit early threat detection, rapid response generation, and effective cooperation.

Laboratory findings have pointed to numerical under-representation as a "threat in the air" that causes women to underperform in quantitative domains, even in the presence of a single man. Chapter 4 was designed to examine whether a similar effect occurs outside the laboratory in ecologically rich environments. Women from a coed versus a single-gender college were assigned to threat and no-threat conditions at a third location. An ANCOVA with math-SAT as a covariate suggested that only the coed women were affected negatively by threat despite their single-gender counterparts' higher levels of math and gender identification; factors linked to heightened threat susceptibility. Following Yzerbyt, Muller, and Judd (2004), findings were qualified to include a math-SAT by stereotype threat interaction, which implied a more nuanced protective effect of single-gender schooling. Results are discussed in context of the cues hypothesis, Integrated Process model of stereotype threat, psychological essentialism, and policy ramifications.

In Chapter 5, the relationships between cognitive self-regulation skills and the Big Five personality traits were examined. Sugiura and Umaoka developed the Cognitive Self-Regulation Skills scale (CSRS) whose items were based on cognitive-behavioral therapy techniques.

The CSRS has two subscales: Logical Analysis and Refraining from Catastrophic Thinking. Examining the scale's relationship to personality traits was expected to provide useful clues to factors facilitating or inhibiting the use of cognitive self-regulation skills.

The CSRS and the Big Five Scale were completed by 485 college students. A joint factor analysis revealed that the CSRS items were almost perfectly subsumed under the Big Five while retaining its two subscales. The items of Logical Analysis were included in Openness and the Refraining from Catastrophic Thinking items loaded negatively on Neuroticism. It is suggested that the intellectual and flexible style (Openness) supports the use of active and objective problem-solving skills as measured by Logical Analysis, and that negative emotionality (Neuroticism) makes it difficult to be detached from negative thinking (the skills represented by Refraining from Catastrophic Thinking).

In: Psychology of Threat
Editors: B. Hunter and T. Romero

ISBN: 978-1-62257-344-8
© 2013 Nova Science Publishers, Inc.

Chapter 1

THE SELF-FORTRESS: MOTIVATIONAL RESPONSES TO THREATS TO THE SELF

Verena Graupmann, Dieter Frey and Bernhard Streicher
Ludwig-Maximilians-Universität München,
Munich, Germany

Abstract

The integrity of the self can be defined as the psychological experience that our actions are sensible and goal directed, that we are in control of them, that our behavior is morally adequate, that we are socially included, that our existence is coherent and continuous. Having self-integrity means dealing with our environment in a way that will lead to positive outcomes.

When self-integrity is threatened we experience a motivation to restore it. Depending on the aspect of integrity that is threatened such motivation is associated with different cognitive, emotional and behavioral responses. These responses can be either defensive or adapting.

Taking a comprehensive perspective to explain how people deal with threats to the self, this chapter subsumes psychological reactions to threats to the self in terms of cognitive dissonance, psychological reactance, self-regulation, self-affirmation, belongingness, fairness, self-esteem and self-continuity.

The Self-Fortress: Motivational Responses to Threats to the Self

1. Self, Self Integrity and its Components

> Ruth, a five year old, approached the psychiatrist with "Are you the bogey man? Are you going to fight my mother? Are you the same mother? Are you the same father? Are you going to be another mother?" and finally screaming in terror, "I am afraid I am going to be someone else" [Bender, 1950, p. 135 as cited in Epstein, 1973].

This quote, describing the loss of self in a schizophrenic child, illustrates the importance of an intact self in a dramatic way. It was used by Epstein (1973) to emphasize the general agreement on the existence of an individual experience of self within the field of psychology.

The child's expression importantly alludes to the social anchorage of a sense of self. In the literature the self has widely been ascribed the function of serving as a guide to efficiently interact with our environment (Epstein, 1973; Mead, 1934; Steele, 1988; Sullivan, 1953). Whereas this is often described as regulating the pleasure/pain balance of the individual, from a *social psychological* view, which we are taking here, we define the function of a sense of self to seeking the best ratio between the pleasure goals of the individual and the goal of remaining a valued interaction partner to relevant others.

The notion of *self-integrity* can be seen as the experience of maintaining this ratio. Self-integrity has been defined as the experience of the own person as adaptively and morally adequate in the sense of competence, coherence, control and free choice (Steele, 1988). In accordance with this view, research on the self in social psychology has identified several working principles of the self. In the following we will focus on *consistency, control, belongingness,* and *continuity* as overarching working principles of the self that relate to many motives and outcomes that research has associated with psychological reactions to self-threat.

A. Consistency

Consistency in daily life relates to the radio weather forecast predicting cold weather and the actual feeling of cold air on your face as you leave the house, the arrival of a bus every morning at the same time and your colleagues greeting you as friendly as they have done the day before. Consistency helps us plan the future, and automatize some of our actions, it makes a highly complex physical and social environment easier to handle. Inconsistency could mean the forecast predicting warm weather and the feeling of cold air, the bus not arriving at the stop this morning, and your colleagues giving you angry looks instead of greeting you. When things are inconsistent we experience a state of alarm and are motivated to find out why, or at least adapt our behavior to the unexpected new reality.

The consistency of the self operates according to the same rules, as we observe ourselves thinking, feeling, and acting. When doing something that is at odds with our internal convictions, or when we do something contradictory to a previously expressed opinion we experience cognitive dissonance (Festinger, 1957). We also feel inconsistent when we are engaging in behavior that is contradictory to our self-integrity in terms of competence (e.g. making a bad decision). Being consistent is important not only to be able to predict our own actions and desires and to ensure adherence to our long term goals. It is also an inherently social motivation, as we have learned that others value consistency in us as interaction partners, as much as we value it in them. Consistency in the social context is a basis for trust in relationships with others and a way of handling a complex social environment by being able to make predictions of other people's reactions.

The psychological mechanisms associated with consistency motivation, namely that once we have adopted a conviction as ours, we experience dissonance when we are about to act or are acting against that conviction, can help us understand the power of moral values as guides for behavior.

B. Control

Having control over outcomes is crucial for the efficient interaction of an individual with the environment. Being able to e.g. control the temperature of a room by using a heater in the winter has immediate effects on wellbeing and in extreme cases, survival. Being able to control things is an important cognition of the self. Therefore, information that threatens this cognition (i.e. information that control is limited or eliminated) should, as threat to integrity, lead to a state of alarm, an emotional state and motivational arousal directed at adjustments of behavior to ensure the regaining of control. The subjective sense of control is therefore important for psychological wellbeing. Illusions of control have been described as part of the mechanisms that are related to mental health (Taylor and Brown, 1988), particularly in comparison with people suffering from depression, who have more realistic perceptions of the actual control they have over outcomes (Alloy and Abramson, 1981). In the extreme form, a sense of loss of control and the feeling that control cannot be retrieved can lead to the generalized notion of learned helplessness (Seligman, 1975): Even if there are ways to control events, they are not perceived and used when too much loss of control has been experienced before.

Control over outcomes is very closely tied to the concept of *freedom*. Reactance theory in particular (Brehm, 1966) proposes the importance of individual freedom and behavioral choices. Freedom in the terms of reactance theory is defined as a person's belief to be able to engage in a certain behavior and to decide on the type of behavior, as well as how it is performed and when. The theory proposes that when a person believes s/he is free to engage in a given behavior, s/he will experience psychological reactance if that freedom is eliminated or threatened. According to Brehm (1966; Brehm and Brehm, 1981), psychological reactance is defined as a motivational state directed toward the re-establishment of the threatened or eliminated freedoms. Reactance should therefore manifest itself in an increased desire to engage in the relevant behavior or actual attempts to engage in it.

Brehm (1966) emphasizes that a loss of freedom should lead to reactance no matter how justified or legitimate the reason, and that only attempts to restore the freedom will be affected by the legitimacy of the restriction. Dickenberger, Gniech, and Grabitz (1993), however hold that the illegitimacy of the restriction is an important factor for the arousal of reactance. Also Gordon (1974) suggests to speak of reactance as a motivation to avoid illegitimate pressures rather than as a motivation to restore freedom. It is expected that reactance is more likely to be experienced when the elimination of the freedom looks illegitimate to the person. On the individual level reactance appears to be an immediate reaction to infringements to freedom (Graupmann and Streicher, 2012).

On the collective level, i.e. in a broader societal context, notions of legitimacy and personal control, make perceptions of *fairness* an important variable for the idea of self. It has been theorized that among other reasons for why people prefer fair conditions over unfair conditions, it is having a guarantee to not be overreached and having the possibility to influence decisions and outcomes. Based on social exchange theory (Thibaut and Kelley, 1959), it is assumed that people show cooperative behavior because they are motivated to gain access to resources (Thibaut and Walker, 1975). The level of cooperative behavior that people show in social contexts depends on the value of the resources they can obtain. To maximize favorable outcomes people are interested in having control over the decisions leading to relevant outcomes. Therefore people favor conditions of fair resource allocations (e.g. unbiased, rule-based procedures) because they guarantee decision control and long-term favorable outcomes (Brett and Goldberg, 1983).

C. Belongingness

We want to be meaningfully connected to other people. Being a part of a group, the *need to belong*, is a powerful motivation (Baumeister and Leary, 1995).

Inclusion, on a very fundamental level means protection, reproduction, and access to shared resources, whereas exclusion, goes along with less security, less resources to access and less opportunities for reproduction (Gruter and Masters, 1986).

The prominent psychological concept of *self-esteem* is seen as a representation of perceiving oneself to be socially accepted, included and adequate (Bednar, Wells, and Peterson, 1989). In particular Leary (1999) suggests that self-esteem as a psychological system has evolved as an alarm system to monitor potential loss of social acceptance leading to exclusion. As a so-called "sociometer" self-esteem has shown to be tied strongly to the need to belong: the sole possibility of rejection reduces state self-esteem. It is theorized that some of the negative outcomes that pursuing self-esteem goals can have in terms of internal integrity (e.g. autonomy, competence; see Crocker and Park, 2004) are due to the overarching goal of being accepted by relevant others (Leary, 1999).

Acceptance by relevant others is a major theme in view on interpersonal feeling, thinking and behaving taken by *social identity* theory (Tajfel, 1978). Social identity is the part of a person's self-concept that relates to the membership in groups. Seeking to maintain a positive social identity by giving positive value to one's own group (ingroup) and distinguishing one's group from other groups (outgroups) is the behavior associated with this part of the self-system. Social and personal identity can be threatened by the social context, e.g. negative behavior of members of the own ingroup, by exclusion from a relevant group or over-inclusion in a stereotyped group, and the responses to such threats are contingent upon the extent of group commitment, i.e. the strength of identification with an ingroup (Ellemers, Spears, and Doosje, 2002).

This strongly relates to the social role of fairness. Fair treatment by groups, authorities or organizations serves as positive identity-relevant information. Conditions of fairness communicate self-relevant information on how much people are respected in a group (Lind and Tyler, 1988) or by an authority (Tyler and Lind, 1992), and how proud they can feel of being a member of that group (Tyler, 1989; Tyler, Degoey, and Smith, 1996). When people are treated fairly they can maintain a positive social identity with their group or the authority (Tyler and Blader, 2000; Tyler and Degoey, 1995; Tyler, 2000). In contrast, unfair treatment leads to lower identification.

D. Continuity

The impact of the idea that our existence is limited is illustrated by very specific reactions upon encountering the notion of death in any form. Terror-Management-Theory (Greenberg, Pyszczynski, and Solomon, 1986; Solomon, Greenberg, and Pyszczynski, 1991) describes these reactions as an attempt to symbolically insist on the continuity of one's own existence by upvaluing one's cultural worldview and values, e.g. by becoming more patriotic.

The motive leading to the behaviors found in response to death reminders represents the desire for *continuity of the self*. Self-continuity or identity continuity is an important motive related to the notion of being the same person over time and integrating change into past and present ideas of the self and how the self relates to others. As exemplified in the example at the beginning of this chapter, this notion is strongly related to basic psychological functioning. There is evidence that self discontinuity is e.g. associated with dissociative disorders (Lampinen, Odergard, and Leding, 2004).

The desire for continuity is further represented in the sentiment of *nostalgia*, defined as a self-relevant positively toned longing for the past (Sedikides, Wildschut, and Baden, 2004). Proneness to nostalgia is associated with being less susceptible to and defensive when confronted with notions of death (Routledge, Arndt, Sedikides, and Wildschut, 2008).

Assimilation and Adaptation in Response to Threats

Comparing the self-concept, i.e. a person's understanding of what defines the own person physically, psychologically and socially in distinction from others, and its contents to a scientific theory Epstein (1973) pointed out that like conservative scientists we try to hold on to the postulates of our self-theory. However, when the empirical evidence that threatens the validity and applicability of our theory become too overwhelming, we integrate the new findings and if need be even change basic postulates of our theory, to keep it functional. The assumption of being an accomplished chef cannot be held after all the friends who have been at ours for dinner, suggest going to a restaurant or bringing take-out the next time they are invited over. In other words, it is possible to apply the Popperian philosophy of science (Popper, 1935) to how we deal with self-knowledge: On the one hand we strive for verification of our self-theory, on the other hand we are led to falsify and thereby improve it to integrate new empirical evidence.

The working principles of the self, which are described above, are heavily guarded and threats cause emotional cognitive and behavioral responses. The responses to threats to self-integrity, even though defensive initially and therefore often leading to changes in perception and evaluation of information, under certain conditions can also be *adapting* to the circumstances, and can lead to innovative changes in the long run. In analogy to Piaget's (1985) theory of children's cognitive development, dealing with threats to the self is thus both assimilation and adaptation.

The Self as a Fortress

The role of the self for the integration of the sense experiences in a way that allows subjectivity is central to the psychological experiences of a person. The neuroscientist Damasio (2010) describes the self as what is (dynamically) added to basic brain processing, so that a conscious mind is at work. The self navigates the person through an abundance of information comprising the present situation, the past and the anticipated future. Given its primal role in our interaction with the world as we experience it, it seems logical that in order to maintain and protect this central relay of information functioning in balance, many mechanisms are at work.

In order to convey this idea of maintenance, protection and integration we choose the metaphor of the self as a fortress. This metaphor conveys the idea that successful integration of self-motives, like consistency, control, belongingness, and continuity, leading to an efficient interaction with the world, means to balance the forces within a stronghold. Forces can be assigned at the different bridges and entrances to the external word, compensate at weak points and respond to threats, much like the structure and functioning of a fortress. Importantly though, a fortress cannot exist independently of its surroundings. It needs to maintain good relationships with the outside world to maintain life on the inside, and sometimes it has to adapt its structure to changes in its surroundings.

A fortress is defined as a military stronghold erected with the idea of protecting the people and resources inside. It is usually built in a place that is hard to reach because it is either separated by water or up on an elevation in the landscape. A fortress mostly has a centripetal structure with the most central parts being the most important, most protected parts. A fortress can have several entrances, e.g. over bridges. Entrances have facilities so that they can be strongly guarded. The outer wall is often combined with a walkway to be used for observation and stationing of defensive forces and it might feature towers for observation. There are usually storage rooms for resources in the more central parts. There are guestrooms, rooms for hospitality and communication, however there is usually also a prison. All of these features can be translated into the functions the self has to employ to protect its central motives and balance.

A safe position, implying consistency and continuity, can be created through self-presentation and status, but also by values and beliefs. The centripetal structure is represented by the most personal emotions and cognitions being at the very core of the self and also being the least likely to be reached and changed quickly. The entrances and bridges as the connections of the self with the environment represent the notion that ideas and persons can enter the fortress and can be integrated or they can be kept at a distance. The walls are the representation of the self in its integrity needing to distinguish self-related information from other information, needing to protect self-motives, but also having to be permeable. The differential way in which the self-concept is separated from others in individualistic and collectivistic cultures, with collectivistic self-concepts being defined by more overlap and more permeable borders as described by Markus and Kitayama (1991) also speaks to this metaphor. The observation structures can be translated in sensitivity for situational and social cues. The defensive structures can be equaled with the actual mechanisms that are triggered once a threat to the self has been detected in the environment. Storage for resources of the self are self-esteem, secure attachment, and coping strategies. Guestrooms and banquet halls represent the parts of the self that are accessible to close others, where the self merges with the other. Prisons represent unresolved conflicts and fears that are maintained but contained and regulated within the self-system.

The overarching theoretical idea is thus, that many self-motives and related outcomes can be traced back to central components of self-integrity threatened. Once a self-threat is detected, a warning system over emotions and motivational states is triggered to maintain self-integrity. These mechanisms are specific in terms of the component of self-integrity that is threatened.

Taking into account the theoretical perspective proposed by Steele (1988) that self-affirmation in another self-domain might be able to compensate or buffer if no other response is available, we argue that within the self system fortress there can be a lot of efficient exchange of resources, as long as the core values and beliefs of the person are clear and unharmed. Additionally the role of specific (e.g. preference for consistency) or more general (neuroticism) *individual* differences as well as *cultural* differences can work as specific or overarching buffers against self-threat.

In the following we describe more specifically threats to self-integrity, the resulting motivational and emotional states that energize reactions on the cognitive and the behavioral level, using the general framework of the self-fortress.

2. Threats to Self Integrity, Resulting Motivational States and Cognitive-Behavioral Outcomes

A. Threats to Consistency: Values and Actions

1. Dissonance as a Threat to Cognitive Balance

Imagine you have been expressing support for a local politician among your friends, very strongly. Also you are the devoted owner of a dog that you like to take on long walks in the forest so it can run freely. One day you read about a law suggested by your favorite politician that prohibits dogs running without a leash in the forests. This causes a clear inconsistency with your support, your identification with that politician, also in your self-presentation to others, and the dog owner aspect of yourself. In other words it is a threat to your self-integrity. In order to resolve cognitive dissonance and restore consistency you might try to put the suggestion of the law in a justifying context and seek out information that supports the view that it is not contrary to your ideas about dog owners' rights or you might change your opinion about the politician (Festinger, 1957), which might again, cause you to selectively seek out information to bolster your opinion shift and bring it in line with your other values. In any case, the arrival of information that is inconsistent with your beliefs is likely to induce a selective search for information to restore consistency. This strategy deals with the threat but results in a biased information search, which can impair impartial consideration of all the relevant information available (Brownstein, 2003; Frey, 1986). A great amount of research looking at how people deal with information once they have taken a position in a decision or opinion issue provides evidence for this bias in order to defend cognitive consistency from contradictory cognitions (for an overview see Frey, 1986).

Aronson (1969) has framed dissonance as a response to a threat to a view of the self as competent and moral, emphasizing its motivational nature in contrast to a purely cognitive conflict. Having the support of a politician as a part of one's self image turns inconsistent information into a threat directed towards the core structure of the self-fortress, leading to a generalized reaction that can involve and bias all the related mechanisms of information processing.

However, when dissonance cannot be reduced because consonant information is not to be found, people do look at dissonant information and are more likely to revise a made decision, i.e. change a behavior, as has been shown in experiments by Festinger himself (Festinger, 1964). This indicates that when maintenance of consistency in a certain domain turns out to not be feasible in the long run, people show adapting behavior in terms of openness to change.

In a similar vein research on ambivalence has shown that when people are aware of their own mixed emotions implied in the contradictory issues at stake, they look at information available in a more balanced manner (Graupmann and Sparks, 2012): Making a decision of where to donate money to, students looked at information inconsistent with their decision with as much interest as at information that supported their decision when they had expressed high ambivalence regarding their decision, while those indicating low ambivalence selectively looked at more supporting information. For those with low ambivalence, a stronger self-involvement could be shown, i.e. for them information inconsistent with their decision is perceived as a threat warded of by a selective exposure to information. Biased treatment of available information can lead to faulty decision making as has been shown in e.g. in research on political decision making (Redlawsk, 2002). Sometimes inconsistent information is crucial and should not be overlooked or moved out of sight. Acknowledging ambivalence moves the issue out of the core of the self. Therefore the threat is not as intimidating to the whole self-system. It can be dealt with by open-mindedly looking at the available information, or in other words, this kind of information can stay in one of the guest rooms instead of being thrown into the prison of the self-fortress.

2. Dissonance as Threat to Moral Integrity

When moral convictions, beliefs that define the greater meaning frame of our acting, are questioned by our own behavior, this can be even more threatening to the self-system than dealing with facts or opinions on day-to-day politics. Imagine yourself as an adamant advocate of recycling in your family, constantly reminding your family members to separate the trash. One day in a rush you don't have time to walk the extra block to the recycling bin and just throw the glass and paper bag into the general waste bin, as one of your family members walks by.

As Stone, Wiegand, Cooper, and Aronson (1997) point out, when made aware of behavior that stands in contrast with advocated values, a person realizes that either the behavior or the advocating of the respective beliefs was false and unprincipled. This should represent a very acute threat to one's sense self-integrity. In their research, participants, who had been asked to give a videotaped speech on the importance of condom use, were then asked to list instances in which they had not conformed with the advocated behavior and failed to use a condom. This clear discrepancy between the expressed moral rule and the own behavior lead to choosing a direct, behavioral way of reducing the threat, i.e. by using the money earned in the study for buying condoms, rather than investing in another good cause. This suggests that when a threat to the self is as menacing as the danger of appearing hypocritical behavioral corrections, even though generally assumed to be last resort, as they are usually associated with the highest effort, are likely to be pursued. Accordingly most energy will be spent on protecting self-integrity in the self-fortress, when the threat is the most direct and cannot easily be resolved otherwise.

On the other hand an intact moral value system as a basis of self-integrity can be a potent buffer against threats to other parts of self-integrity. Research on self-affirmation has e.g. shown that an opportunity to affirm central moral values led to less biased processing of counter-attitudinal information (Cohen, Aronson, and Steele, 2000) and less forced-compliance induced attitude change (Steele and Liu,

1983). Self-affirmation has further been shown to make people more open to relevant but threatening health risk information (Sherman, Nelson, and Steele, 2000; Harris and Napper, 2005), and to even be an important psychosomatic factor in the healing process of cancer patients (Creswell, Lam, Stanton, Taylor, Bower, and Sherman, 2007). Opportunities for self affirmation in these studies are often established by letting participants write about why their most important value is so relevant to them. These findings give self-affirmation a meaningful role in applied contexts and imply that the self-fortress, when built around a solid center can be very flexible in dealing with various types of threats. Self-affirmation can therefore also be seen as facilitating adapting in contrast to defensive behavior.

B. Threats to Control: Restoring Freedom and Fair Outcomes

1. Threats to Freedom: Reactance

When the passenger next to me on an airplane takes over the armrest between the two seats, it becomes more important to me. All of a sudden resting my arm becomes a strong desire, space seems to be limited, and waiting for the person to move the arm becomes the focus of attention. A freedom of choice, even if not made use of before, can become a self-related issue, and its retrieval a motivational force, after it is threatened or eliminated: Freedom in the sense of having the control over outcomes is crucial for the distinction of the self from others as well as for the integration of aspects of the self (Johnson and Buboltz, 2000).

Research on psychological reactance has produced a great array of findings showing how the motivation to maintain personal freedom leads to increased desire or actual attempts to engage in the relevant behavior (for an overview see Miron and Brehm, 2006). This has been shown e.g. for consumer behavior (Weiner and Brehm, 1966): bread sales were lower when it was advertised with the choice-restricting "You must buy this bread", compared to "Please try this bread". Complying with rules, more people wrote graffiti on a bathroom wall when there was a sign saying "Do not write on these walls under any circumstances" and less when it said "Please do not write on these walls" (Pennebaker and Sander, 1976).

Particularly research looking at differences in reactance between people with Western (more individualistic) versus Eastern (more collectivistic) cultural backgrounds however, has shown that these can be traced back to differences in the culturally determined self-construal (Jonas, et al. 2009), thereby emphasizing the origin of reactance in a self-motive. Participants from individualistic cultural backgrounds showed more reactance when a personal freedom was restricted than people from collectivistic cultural backgrounds. This could be explained by the differences in the self-construal. Collectivistic participants reacted with more reactance only when a collective freedom was threatened (i.e. a freedom of pertaining to the whole group they belonged to), while individualistic participants showed similar levels of reactance in both cases. Differences in the individualistic versus collectivistic (independent vs. interdependent) self-construal were associated with reactance, indicating that a threat to freedom causes reactance when it is relevant to the self-construal.

Reactance is an easily triggered motivational state that ensures control over outcomes when external pressures appear to interfere with personal goals of freedom, making it an obvious defense mechanism in the self-fortress. Due to the existential nature of having control, psychological reactance as an immediate and automatic reaction to threats to freedom is a mechanism that is strongly tied to protecting self-integrity.

However, when there is no expectation of future control there is less resistance against threats to freedom. Wortman and Brehm (1975) have established a theoretical model to account for both the situations in which people will try restore control or freedom and the situations in which they will not. They proposed that when a situation is characterized by uncontrollability, people will show resistance against the loss of freedom in the form of psychological reactance. However, when the situation continues to be uncontrollable and there is no indication that there will be control in the future, people resign, i.e. lose the motivation to change the situation and enter into the state that has been described as learned helplessness by Seligman (1975) that is associated with cognitive deficits and even depression. This model manages to integrate the otherwise contradictory predictions of reactance theory and the learned helpless model into a theory of controllability expectations. Whereas this model takes the effects of expectations of uncontrollability to the extremes, it is important to consider situational variables that might lead to adaptation to a situation without the individual withdrawing from the situation psychologically and resigning into helplessness. In fact, the level of reactance should depend also on the social context. There are conditions in which people do not react only defensively, but take into account circumstantial information, e.g. how *legitimate* a restriction to freedom is (Grabitz-Gniech, 1971). In particular in groups and in situations of restricted resources the restriction of a personal freedom can be seen as legitimate in order to maintain social norms and effective cooperation, which in turn is beneficial for all group members on the long run. Accordingly, notions of fair outcomes and thus of living together with others in a larger societal context reduce reactance responses (Graupmann and Streicher, 2012). This provides further evidence for the flexibility and of how the self deals with threat, taking into account the balance of individual wellbeing and social balance, which is important for individual wellbeing in the long run.

2. Threats to Trust in the Social System: Fairness of Outcomes

An abundance of social interactions are associated with the uncertainty whether one will profit from this interaction or one will be overreached. On the one hand, if people identify for example with authorities and obey the roles of a group, organization or society, personal benefits and favorable outcomes can be achieved. When following social norms people simultaneously count on reciprocity: That the norms will not only be applied in the favor of others but in their favor as well, and that they can have trust in the social system. On the other hand, hierarchical and dependent situations make one vulnerable to exploitation. Speaking in line with the fortress metaphor: Is it beneficial to interact with outsiders (e.g. trading food with merchants) or dangerous, because they might smuggle in the infamous Trojan horse? This fundamental social dilemma is particularly significant in hierarchical situations (e.g. supervisor-employee-relation), situations with restricted resources (e.g. access to goods), and situations of high personal importance (e.g. romantic relationship). The self-threatening aspects of the fundamental social dilemma can be effectively buffered when one can trust the interaction partners that they will not misemploy ones dependency. Having trust in social systems (i.e. trusting not being exploited) is a fundamental precondition of human cooperation, prosperity, and the establishment of complex, stable and benevolent societies in general. Accordingly the loss of trust in social systems, regardless of whether a dyadic interaction or a more complex social unity is concerned, is self-threatening.

Unfortunately, to build up trust needs time and repeated interactions and is never totally reliable. Therefore, people seek information on the trustworthiness of relevant others and the social system. One important proxy on how trustworthy social systems are is to find out how fair individuals are treated by this system and how much fair resource allocations are applied (e.g. everybody gets his/her bit) (Lind, 2001; Van den Bos, Lind, and Wilke, 2001). In general a fair allocation of resources is established when accepted norms are applied to reach the outcome. Such norms include the equity-principle (i.e. the better the performance in relation to others the higher the outcome), the equality-principle (i.e. everybody receives the same outcome), and the need-principle (i.e. those needy receive higher outcomes) (Deutsch, 1975). People use accessible fairness information about the social system as a proxy for its trustworthiness and relay on this fairness heuristic in decisions concerning the social dilemma. If information on the fairness of outcomes is sketchy, other forms of fairness information are used to judge the trustworthiness of the social system (Van den Bos, Lind, Vermunt, and Wilke, 1997). In this context one particularly important fairness information refers to the fairness of procedures that lead to a certain outcome. In a wider sense fair procedures comprise among others the opportunity to voice one opinion, lack of bias, correction of the decision, accuracy of information, and are respectful treatment (Bies and Moag, 1986; Leventhal, 1980). Interestingly, people are more likely to accept disadvantaging outcomes if they feel treated fairly, are more likely to comply with decisions made by others, and are more committed to such decisions (for an overview, see Van den Bos, 2005). This so called fair process effect can be explained with the positive self-relevant information of a fair treatment and procedure: Being an important and respected member of the social system. Overall, the positive reactions to fair procedures even in the face of unfair or disadvantaging outcomes represent another example for the two-sidedness of the self in terms of defense and adaptation.

C. Threats to Belonging and Social Standing: Self-Esteem and Social Identity

1. Threats to Self Esteem

Failure in any domain of life can pose an acute threat to self-esteem: Not passing an important test, separating from a partner, being rejected by a potential partner, not receiving an expected promotion. When experiencing failure we can experience a temporary drop in self-esteem, as also our social standing, i.e. high evaluation by others seems endangered (Leary, Tambor, Terdal, and Downs, 1995). Focusing on self-evaluation maintenance strategies, Tesser and colleagues (Tesser, Crepaz, Collins, Cornell, and Beach, 2000) explain that people have different efficient ways of dealing with threats to self-esteem that can substitute each other: Being threatened by failure in a self-esteem relevant domain, they argue, people can try to perform better in that domain (performance), they can change the domain of comparison with others, or they can reevaluate and reduce the relevance of the domain in question.

Maintenance of self-esteem appears, at least in individualistic societies, a very important psychological task, with self-esteem being associated with higher self-confidence, happiness and strong initiative (McFarlin and Blascovich, 1981; Baumeister, Campbell, Krueger, and Vohs, 2003). Similarly positive illusions about the self have been associated with enhanced mental health (Taylor and Brown, 1988). However, there is a lot of evidence that *pursuing* self-esteem can also have costs to the individual (Baumeister, et al. 2003; Crocker and Park,

2004): With self-esteem being closely tied to approval from others, pursuing self-esteem can compromise long-term goals of the individual (e.g. performing well in college), when short term goals related to social standing (e.g. going out for drinks every night) are deemed more important. This is especially the case for people with low trait self-esteem, as they are chronically looking for more social acceptance, whereas those with higher trait self-esteem are more likely to maintain self-esteem by competence and achievement (Blaine and Crocker, 1993).

Also here, it becomes obvious that threats to self-integrity can be met not only defensively by focusing on pure self-enhancement goals when self-esteem is at stake. In certain situations personal growth and being socially connected emerge as long term goals for the self that can only be met by facing negative feedback related to the self realistically to adapt and improve.

The theories people have about the self can have an impact on how they deal with threats to self-esteem. The research conducted by Carol Dweck has consistently shown, that those who believe that ability can be learned (incremental theory) are more likely to persist after failure, whereas those who believe that ability is unchangeable (entity theory) are more likely to feel worthless after failure and give up (Dweck, 2000).

Seeing self-esteem as a sociometer (Leary, 1999), social exclusion emerges as the most *direct* threat to self-esteem. Not surprisingly, apart from being avoided indirectly through all other ways of self-esteem pursuit, does actual exclusion lead to dramatic consequences: Social exclusion activates the same neuronal alarm system as physical pain (Eisenberger, Liebermann, and Williams, 2003). Over time social exclusion has shown to have the same negative health outcomes as smoking or diabetes (House, Landis, and Umberson, 1988). When excluded people report lower levels of the four basic needs belonging, control, self-esteem, and meaningful existence even if the exclusion was conducted by a computer (Zadro, Williams, and Richardson, 2004).

In collectivistic societies researchers find tendencies for self-criticism and self-improvement rather than self-enhancement (e.g. Heine, Takata, and Lehman, 2000; for an overview: Heine and Hamamura, 2007), however, it might be subsumed under the same idea: achieving self regard, even if cultural circumstance determine how such a self-regard is achieved and what makes is functional within a culture (Heine, Lehmann, Markus and Kitayama, 1999). Importantly however, the self-regard is regulated and guarded, across cultures.

It has been shown across cultures, however, that unfair decision making procedures and unfair interactional treatment represent a self-threat, because this kind of unfairness carries the message that one is not a valued member of the group and one's belonging to the group is at stage. On the contrary fair treatment like the ability to voice one's opinion, respectful and honoring interactions, and accurate and timely information helps the self to maintain a positive self-value and high levels of self-esteem in even otherwise threatening situations (Lind, Tyler, and Huo, 1997)

The gauging of social standing in the self-fortress and – when a threat is identified – the subsequent shift in motivation can clearly be traced back to the survival function of being a valued member of a group, threat of exclusion – directly or indirectly by a threat to self-esteem is therefore protected by a highly sensitive system of regulation, and if inclusion is at stake people are likely to throw internal consistency or freedom of choice over the fortress wall. This has become very clear already in studies conducted by Asch in the nineteen-fifties (1951/1956), where participants, when faced with a group of others coming to wrong conclusions, adjusted their own, correct, judgment and perception of the situation to not stick out. Alternatively, however, one can imagine that a well-founded value system can counteract rash impulses to conform with others in order to protect social standing and instead help a person to focus on the larger perspective of self integrity.

2. Threats to the Ingroup as Threats to the Self

Why does reading about misbehavior of one's countrymen (e.g. showing disrespectful behavior to another culture while vacationing abroad) feel worse when reading about it in the international press than when reading about it in the local newspaper? When we read about such things within the context of our own country, we can distinguish ourselves and define those who misbehave as belonging to different social group, and there is little threat to our own social identity. When we read about such events in the international press we realize that in that context we are considered a member of the ingroup the misbehaving individual is considered a part of, therefore it is more likely to be experienced as a threat to the social self.

The social part of a person's identity, i.e. the group memberships can be seen as the aspect of social standing we share with others. In that sense, social identity can be the more stable part of self-esteem that can compensate for individual failure and sense of loss of control. When threatened individually, identification with ingroups becomes stronger. However, social identity is also the part of our identity that we have less individual control over, therefore identification with an ingroup is varied according to situations. Optimal Distinctiveness Theory (ODT, Brewer 1991, 2003) is a theoretical framework to make predictions about the direction of an individual's behavior toward ingroups and outgroups: Given that people have concurring needs to belong to and be distinct from others, people monitor their assimilation to and distinctiveness from others. They do this in order to reach an optimal, functional level of distinctiveness and choose their social identities accordingly. It is assumed that it is a characteristic of all societies that the needs for both individual and collective identity are met. However, in different cultures the meaning of ingroup is shaped differently (Triandis, 1995), which results in different needs for distinctiveness: Individualists are be more likely refer to close others for needs of belonging *and* distinction, whereas collectivists pursue distinctiveness needs by being distinct from outgroup members rather than from ingroup members. This conclusion corresponds to a taxonomy proposed by Hornsey and Jetten (2004), distinguishing the pursuit of affiliation and distinctiveness motives on the individual (within-group) level versus on the collective (between-groups) level. In accordance with this perspective, differences have been found by Brewer and Roccas (2001): In their studies individuals holding individualistic values identified with larger, less distinct groups (allowing within-group distinction), while those holding collectivistic values identified more strongly with groups that were smaller and more distinct from outgroups. Looking at psychological reactance after choice was restricted Graupmann, Jonas, Meier, Hawelka and Aichhorn (2012) found collectivists to show reactance only when a threat came from an outgroup, while complying with restrictions from the ingroup, whereas individualists, in accordance with a greater need to be distinct from ingroup members, showed more resistance against restrictions from ingroup members and even conformed with restrictions from outgroup members (as if to show even more distinction from the ingroup).

Under which circumstances are we less defensive and more likely to integrate new aspects to our social identity? Roccas and Brewer (2002) propose that being aware of the complexity of one's social identity, i.e. the many and different groups that one might belong to and that do not fully overlap (e.g. belonging to the ingroup of women and belonging to the ingroup of scientists) leads to more tolerance towards outgroup members.

Group memberships can be a way to maintain self-integrity and they are crucial as they can represent the actual access we have to resources and protection from our social environment. In terms of the self-fortress social identity relates to the way the fortress is embedded in a "political" context, how connected with other, greater structures it is, how welcoming it is to guests and ambassadors and how eagerly it maintains relationships with others from a potential ingroup. Looking at the more interdependent self in terms of Markus and Kitayama (1991), where close others are included more permanently in the individual's self-concept, one can even imagine the self as a fortress constantly and openly connected with other fortresses.

D. Threats to Continuity: Self over Time

1. Self-continuity Theory

It can be extremely unsettling when another person insists on remembering a situation from the past that includes us, but that we cannot remember. Having a sense of continuity is important for navigating the self through time. It is a part of William' (1890/1950) idea of the self as providing continuity. Continuity can be threatened by a disconnect in the past, i.e. a memory that is missing, a sense of unconnectedness in one's life story, by e.g. a traumatic event or a big change in life circumstances (e.g. starting a new life in a new country as a refugee). Autobiographical memory is an important part of the content and the continuity of personal identity (Addis and Tippett, 2008). Continuous self-narratives provide coherence and meaningful connections between past and present selves and help to envision a future self. People who lose autobiographical memory, e.g. amnesia patients (Tulving, 1985), have difficulty imagining the future. People who indicated feeling very close and connected to their future self, on the other hand, showed more capacity for delay of gratification, i.e. were better at securing positive future outcomes for themselves (Ersner-Hershfield, Garton, Ballard, Samanez-Larkin and Knutson, 2009).

2. Nostalgia

Nostalgia, the state of longing for the positive aspects of the past can be seen as a means to deal with big life transitions, when there is danger of losing continuity. For centuries nostalgia has been associated with homesickness (for a review see Sedikides, et al., 2004), appearing in stressful situations of transition and leaving a familiar home environment. Looking at studies that show the positive emotional effect engaging nostalgic thinking has on mood, as well as the findings of people showing more nostalgic thinking to compensate negative moods (Wildschut, Sedikides, Arndt, and Routledge, 2006), nostalgia emerges as a regulation strategy when continuity is threatened: Nostalgic longing guides the self to retrieve autobiographical memory to maintain a coherent, positive narrative and should in turn allow better adaptation of the self to the present situation and adequate planning of future behavior. Nostalgic behavior has further been assumed to also strengthen social ties and thus the social definition of the self (Wildschut, et al. 2006). The idea that nostalgia as a self-mechanism ensures the continuity between past and present selves (Sedikides, Wildschut, Arndt, and Routledge, 2008) and the omnipresence of nostalgia in culture and thinking emphasizes the importance continuity has for personal and social aspects of self-integrity.

3. Time Perspective

Self-continuity is permanently threatened by the knowledge of inevitability of death. In this context Carstensen, Isaacowitz and Charles (1999) describe the age-related differences in how time is perceived: Older people view time as more limited (being more aware of their life's eventual ending), while younger people see time as more unlimited. Accordingly older people engage in more emotion regulation in interpersonal relationships as immediate emotional goals are more relevant to them than are long term goals (Carstensen, Fung and, Charles, 2003). However, individual differences in temporal perspective are also associated with differences in social motives independent of age (Fung, Lai, Ng, 2001). An expansive time perspective is associated with the overall goal to acquire accurate information about the world, in order to successfully pursue long term goals. A limited time perspective is associated with the goal of positive emotional experiences in interpersonal interactions (Carstensen et al., 2003). In addition it has been shown that the influence of temporal perspective on social goals affects subsequent attitude adaptation to relevant social groups (De Wall, Visser, and Levitan, 2006). Those with an induced more limited time perspective went along with group consensus more than those who were led to see time as more expansive. This suggests that the need to belong to a social group, and thus the threat of exclusion from a group, is affected by temporal perspective, pointing to the idea of fluency of forces in the self-fortress: When continuity is threatened by a chronically limited time perspective, regulation might occur over strengthening immediate belongingness needs.

4. Terror-Management Theory

In research on terror-management this perspective is taken to a more existential, general level: When people are reminded of their own death, strengthening their ties to the bigger context they are a part of, i.e. their culture, by affirming or defending their cultural worldview is the way to deal with this threat to continuity (Pyszczynski, Solomon, Greenberg, and Maxfield, 2006). When consciously aware of death, people employ proximal coping strategies reducing the anxiety by e.g. emphasizing their physical health (Pyszczynski, Greenberg, and Solomon, 1999). However, in most instances in everyday life notions of death are not consciously worked through and people deal with the existential fear evoked with more overarching, distal defenses: By believing in an afterlife and thereby religiously and philosophically striving for immortality, or by focusing on extensions of the own existence represented by lasting achievements, one's

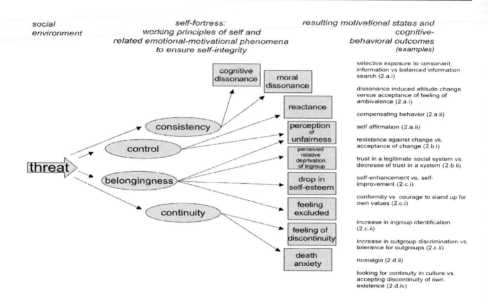

Figure 1. Summary of the self-fortress reactions to threat to self-integrity.

culture, one's children, i.e. by insisting on symbolic immortality (Burke, Martens, and Faucher, 2010). These defenses are based on the validity of a person's cultural worldview. Terror Management theory (TMT) explains human investment in belief-systems that bolster cultural worldviews with the motivation to cope with death anxiety (Solomon, et al. 1991). Research on TMT has consistently shown that there is an association between death-related thoughts and subsequent reactions that defend, affirm, or strengthen cultural worldviews (Burke, et al., 2010). When mortality is salient people indicate for stronger identification with national symbols (Landau, et al. 2004), upvalue their ingroup (Harmon-Jones, Greenberg, Solomon, and Simon, 1996), and punish behavior that deviates from the cultural norm more strongly (Lieberman, Arndt, Personius, and Cook, 2001). However, also self-esteem has shown to work as anxiety buffer against threats caused by mortality salience (Harmon-Jones, Simon, Greenberg, Pyszczynski, and McGregor, 1997), once again suggesting a flexibility of the self-system in dealing with threats to self-integrity. Especially when taking into account the rituals and cultural references in literature, music and painting, made to death, it is apparent that in the domain of continuity, too, defensive reactions and attempts to integrate potentially threatening information for the purpose of a more stable self-fortress, stand side by side.

Summary and Conclusion

In this chapter we aimed to give an overview over threats to the self from a social psychological perspective. Subsuming self-motives under the concept of the integrity of the self, we based our argument on the idea that self-motives have the function to set the individual into action whenever the efficient interaction with the social environment is endangered. We focused on consistency, control, belongingness and continuity as working principles of the self, related to motivated reactions to threat that ensure self-integrity. The metaphor of the self-fortress pays heed to the notion that self-integrity plays a vital role for the psychological functioning of a person and is thus guarded by an array of mechanisms that are triggered when an event goes counter a central self motive. The motives are related to specific aspects of the self, but the common goal is at the center of the fortress structure. This implies the possibility for fluid compensation, as described, e.g. in the role of self-esteem as a buffer, when continuity is threatened.

Throughout the evidence for how the self deals with threats, there is the finding that even though there is an initial inertia of holding on to established ideas about the self and defending basic expectations of consistency, control, belongingness and continuity, there is also insight into the circumstances and adaptation to in favor of long term goals. When there is no way to assimilate the world according to our expectations, we can adapt our thinking and our evaluations. This flexibility and openness to change allows for more stability of the self-fortress in a complex and constantly changing environment.

As crucial as it is to know about the defenses that the self-fortress has in store when threatened by change or negative feedback, as important it is also to know the potential for integration and expansion in social interactions. As the research has shown again and again in different areas of self-motives (self-affirmation, self esteem, social identity, etc.), when the core of the self related to basic values and needs remains intact, there is more openness to information that would otherwise lead to defense reactions and be blocked out.

References

Addis, D. R. and Tippett, L.J. (2008). The contributions of autobiographical memory to the content and continuity of self: a social-cognitive neuroscience approach. In F. Sani (Ed.), Self-Continuity: *Individual and Collective Perspectives* (pp. 71-84). New York: Psychology Press.

Alloy, L. B., and Abramson, L. Y. (1982). Learned helplessness, depression, and the illusion of control. *Journal of Personality and Social Psychology,* 42, 1114–1126.

Aronson, E. (1969). A theory of cognitive dissonance: A current perspective. In L.Berkowitz (Ed.), *Advances in experimental social psychology* (Vol. 4, pp. 1-34). New York: Academic Press.

Asch, S. E. (1951). Effects of group pressure upon the modification and distortion of judgment. In H. Guetzkow (ed.) *Groups, leadership and men.* Pittsburgh, PA: Carnegie Press.

Asch, S. E. (1956). Studies of independence and conformity: A minority of one against a unanimous majority. *Psychological Monographs,* 70 (9), Whole no. 416.

Baumeister, R. F., Campbell, J. D., Krueger, J. I., and Vohs, K. D. (2003). Does high self-esteem cause better performance, interpersonal success, happiness, or healthier lifestyles? *Psychological Science in the Public Interest, 4,* 1-44.

Baumeister, R. F. and Leary, M. R. (1995). The Need to Belong: Desire for interpersonal attachments as a fundamental human motivation. *Psychological Bulletin,* 117, 497-529.

Bednar, R. L., Wells, M. G., and Peterson, S. R. (1989). *Self-esteem: Paradoxes and innovations in clinical theory and practice.* Washington, DC: American Psychological Association.

Bies, R. J., and Moag, J. F. (1986). Interactional justice: Communication criteria of fairness. In R. J. Lewicki, B. H. Sheppard and M. H. Bazerman (Eds.), *Research on negotiations in organizations* (Vol. 1, pp. 43-55). Greenwich, CT: JAI Press.

Blaine, B., and Crocker, J. (1993). Self-esteem and self-serving biases in reactions to positive and negative events: An integrative review. In R. E Baumeister (Ed.), *Self-esteem: The puzzle of low self-regard* (pp. 55-85). New York: Plenum Press.

Brehm, J. W. (1966). *A theory of psychological reactance.* New York: Academic Press.

Brehm, S. S. and Brehm, J. W. (1981). *Psychological reactance. A theory of freedom and control.* New York, Academic Press.

Brett, J. M., and Goldberg, S. B. (1983). Mediator-advisors: A new third-party role. In M. H. Bazerman and R. J. Lewicki (Eds.), *Negotiations in organizations* (pp. 165-176). Beverly Hills, CA: Sage.

Brewer, M. B. (1991). The social self: On being the same and different at the same time. *Personality and Social Psychology Bulletin,* 17, 475-482.

Brewer, M. B. (2003). Optimal Distinctiveness, Social Identity, and the Self. In M. Leary and J. Tangney (Eds.), *Handbook of Self and Identity*. (pp 480-491) New York: Guilford Press.

Brewer, M. B., and Roccas, S. (2001). Individual values, social identity, and optimal distinctiveness. In C. Sedikides and M. Brewer (Eds.), *Individual self, relational self, collective self* (pp. 219-237). Philadelphia: Psychology Press.

Brownstein, A. L. (2003). Biased Predecision Processing, *Psychological Bulletin*, 12, 545-568.

Burke, B.L., Martens, A. and Faucher, E.H. (2010) Two Decades of Terror Management Theory: A Meta-Analysis of Mortality Salience Research. *Personality and Social Psychology Review*, 14, 155-195.

Carstensen, L.L., Fung, H. and Charles, S. (2003) Socioemotional selectivity theory and the regulation of emotion in the second half of life. *Motivation and Emotion*, 27, 103-123.

Carstensen, L.L., Isaacowitz, D. and Charles, S.T. (1999). Taking time seriously: A theory of socioemotional selectivity. *American Psychologist*, 54, 165-181.

Cohen, G. L., Aronson, J., and Steele, C. M. (2000). When beliefs yield to evidence: Reducing biased evaluation by affirming the self. *Personality and Social Psychology Bulletin*, 26, 1151–1164.

Creswell, J. D., Lam, S., Stanton, A. L., Taylor, S.E., Bower, J. E., and Sherman, D. K. (2007). Does self-affirmation, cognitive processing, or discovery of meaning explain cancer-related health benefits of expressive writing? *Personality and Social Psychology Bulletin*, 33, 238-250.

Crocker, J., and Park, L. E. (2004). The costly pursuit of self-esteem. *Psychological Bulletin*, 130, 392-414.

Damasio, A. (2010). *Self comes to Mind*. Toronto: Random House.

DeWall, C. N., Visser, P. S., and Levitan, L. C. (2006). Openness to attitude change as a function of temporal perspective. *Personality and Social Psychology Bulletin*, 32, 1010-1023.

Deutsch, M. (1975). Equity, equality, and need: What determines which value will be used as the basis of distributive justice? *Journal of Social Issues*, 31, 137-149.

Dickenberger, D., Gniech, G., Grabitz, H.-J. (1993): Die Theorie der psychologischen Reaktanz (The theory of psychological reactance). In: Frey, D., Irle, M. (Eds.). *Theorien der Sozialpsychologie, Band I: Kognitive Theorien*, (pp. 243-273), Bern-Göttingen-Toronto-Seattle: Hans Huber.

Dweck, C. S. (2000). *Self-theories: Their role in motivation, personality, and development*. Philadelphia: Taylor and Francis/Psychology Press.

Eisenberger, N. I., Lieberman, M. D., and Williams, K. D. (2003). Does exclusion hurt? An fMRI study of social exclusion. *Science*, 302, 290-292.

Ellemers, N., Spears, R. Doosje, B. (2002). *Self and Social Identity. Annual Review of Psychology*, 53, 161-186.

Epstein, S. (1973). The self-concept revisited: Or a theory of a theory. *American Psychologist*, 28, 404-416.

Ersner-Hershfield, H., Garton, M. T., Ballard, K., Samanez-Larkin, G. R., Knutson., B. (2009). Don't stop thinking about tomorrow: Individual differences in future self-continuity account for saving. *Judgment and Decision Making*, 4, 280-286.

Festinger, L. (1957). *A theory of cognitive dissonance*. Stanford: Stanford University Press.

Festinger, L. (1964). *Conflict, Decision, and Dissonance*. London: Travistock.

Frey, D. (1986). Recent research on selective exposure to information. *Advances in experimental social psychology*, 19, 41-80.

Fung, H. H., Lai, P., and Ng, R. (2001). Age differences in social preferences among Taiwanese and mainland Chinese: The role of perceived time. *Psychology and Aging*, 16, 351–356. Gordon (1974)

Grabitz,-Gniech, G. (1971): Some restrictive conditions for the occurrence of psychological reactance. *Journal of Personality and Social Psychology*, 19, 188-196.

Graupmann, V., and Sparks, P. (2012) *Decidedly Undecided - Ambivalence and dissonance in decision-making*. Manuscript submitted for publication.

Graupmann, V., and Streicher, B. (2012) *An evolution-of-society view of social influence: Psychological reactions to freedom restrictions and unfairness*. Unpublished manuscript.

Graupmann, V., Jonas, E., Meier, E., Hawelka, S., and Aichhorn, M. (2012). Reactance, the self and its group: When threats to freedom come from the in-group vs. the out-group. *European Journal of Social Psychology*, 42, 164-173.

Greenberg, J., Pyszczynski, T., and Solomon, S. (1986). The causes and consequences of a need for self-esteem: A terror management theory. In R. F. Baumeister (Ed.*), Public Self and Private Self* (pp. 189–212). New York: Springer.

Gruter, M. and Masters, R. (1986). Ostracism as a social and biological phenomenon: an introduction. *Ethology and Sociobiology*, 7, 149-158.

Harmon-Jones, E., Greenberg, J., Solomon, S., and Simon, L. (1996). The effects of mortality salience on intergroup bias between minimal groups. *European Journal of Social Psychology*, 26, 677-681.

Harmon-Jones, E., Simon, L., Greenberg, J., Pyszczynski, T., Solomon, S., and McGregor, H. (1997). Terror management theory and self-esteem: Evidence that increased self-esteem reduces mortality salience effects. *Journal of Personality and Social Psychology, 72*, 24-36.

Harris, P. R., and Napper, L. (2005). Self-affirmation and the Biased Processing of Threatening Health-Risk Information. *Personality and Social Psychology Bulletin, 31*, 1250-1263.

Heine, S.J., and Hamamura, T. (2007). In search of East Asian self-enhancement. *Personality and Social Psychology Review, 11*, 1-24

Heine, S. J., Lehman, D. R., Markus, H. R., and Kitayama, S. (1999). Is there a universal need for positive self-regard? *Psychological Review, 106*, 766-794.

Heine, S. J., Takata, T., and Lehman, D. R. (2000). Beyond self-presentation: Evidence for Japanese self-criticism. *Personality and Social Psychology Bulletin, 26*, 71-78.

Hornsey, M.J. and Jetten, J. (2004) The individual within the group: Balancing the need to belong with the need to be different, *Personality and Social Psychology Review, 8*, 248–264.

House, J. S., Landis, K. R., and Umberson, D. (1988). Social relationships and health. *Science, 241*, 540–545.

James, W. (1950/1890). *Principles of psychology*. New York: Dover.

Johnson, P., and Buboltz, W. C. (2000). Differentiation of self and psychological reactance. *Contemporary Family Therapy, 22*, 91-102.

Jonas, E., Graupmann, V., Kayser, D. N., Zanna, M., Traut-Mattausch, E., and Frey, D. (2009). Culture, self, and the emergence of reactance: Is there a "universal" freedom? *Journal of Experimental Social Psychology, 45*, 1068-1080.

Lampinen, J. M., Odegard, T. N., and Leding, J. K. (2004). Diachronic disunity. In D. R. Beike, J. M. Lampinen, and D. A. Behrend (Eds.), *The self in memory* (pp. 227–253). New York: Psychology Press.

Landau, M. J., Solomon, S., Greenberg, J., Cohen, F., Pyszczynski, T., Arndt, J., et al. (2004). Deliver us from evil: The effects of mortality salience and reminders of 9/11 on support for President George W. Bush. *Personality and Social Psychology Bulletin, 30*, 1136 –1150.

Leary, M. R. (1999). The social and psychological importance of selfesteem. In R. M. Kowalski and M. R. Leary (Eds.), *The social psychology of emotional and behavioral problems: Interfaces of social and clinical psychology* (pp. 197-221). Washington, DC: American Psychological Association.

Leary, M. R., Tambor, E. S., Terdal, S. K., and Downs, D. L. (1995). Self esteem as an interpersonal monitor: The sociometer hypothesis. *Journal of Personality and Social Psychology*, 68, 518-530.

Leventhal, G. S. (1980). What should be done with equity theory? New approaches to the study of fairness in social relationships. In K. J. Gergen, M. S. Greenberg and R. H. Willis (Eds.), *Social exchange: Advances in theory and research* (pp. 27-55). New York: Plenum.

Lieberman, J. D., Arndt, J., Personius, J., and Cook, A. (2001). Vicarious annihilation: The effect of mortality salience on perceptions of hate crimes. *Law and Human Behavior*, 25, 547-566.

Lind, E. A. (2001). Fairness heuristic theory: Justice judgments as pivotal cognitions in organizational relations. In J. Greenberg and R. Cropanzano (Eds.), *Advances in organization justice* (pp. 56-88). Lexington, MA: New Lexington.

Lind, E. A., and Tyler, T. R. (1988). *The social psychology of procedural justice.* New York: Plenum Press.

Lind, E. A., Tyler, T. R., and Huo, Y. J. (1997). Procedural context and culture: Variation in the antecedents of procedural justice judgments. *Journal of Personality and Social Psychology*, 73, 767-780.

Markus, H. R., and Kitayama, S. (1991). Culture and the self: Implications for cognition, emotion, and motivation. *Psychological Review*, 98, 224-253.

McFarlin, D. B., and Blascovich, J. (1981). Effects of self-esteem and performance feedback on future affective preferences and cognitive expectations. *Journal of Personality and Social Psychology*, 40, 521-531.

Mead, G. H. (1934) *Mind, self, and society.* Chicago: University of Chicago Press.

Miron, A. M., and Brehm, J. W. (2006). Reactance theory – 40 years later. *Zeitschrift für Sozialpsychologie*, 37, 9–18.

Pennebaker, J. W., and Sander, D. Y. (1976). American graffiti: Effects of authority and reactance arousal. *Personality and Social Psychology Bulletin*, 3, 264–267.

Piaget, J. (1985). *The Equilibration of Cognitive Structures: The Central Problem of Intellectual Development.* Chicago: University of Chicago Press.

Popper, K. (1935), *Logik der Forschung.* Springer: Wien.

Pyszczynski, T., Greenberg, J., and Solomon, S. (1999). A dual-process model of defense against conscious and unconscious death-related thoughts: An extension of terror management theory. *Psychological Review*, 106, 835-845.

Pyszczynski, T., Greenberg, J., Solomon, S., and Maxfield, M. (2006). On the unique psychological import of the human awareness of mortality: Theme and variations. *Psychological Inquiry*, 17, 328-356.

Redlawsk, D. P. (2002). Hot cognition or cool consideration? Testing the effects of motivated reasoning on political decision making. *Journal of Politics, 64,* 1021-1044.

Roccas, S., and Brewer, M. B. (2002). Social identity complexity. *Personality and Social Psychology Review, 6,* 88-106.

Routledge, C., Arndt, J., Sedikides, C., and Wildschut, T. (2008). A blast from the past: The terror management function of nostalgia. *Journal of Experimental Social Psychology, 44,* 132-140.

Sedikides, C., Wildschut, T, and Baden, D. (2004). Nostalgia: Conceptual issues and existential functions. In J. Greenberg, S. Koole, and T. Pyszczynski (Eds.), *Handbook of experimental existential psychology* (pp. 200-214). New York, NY: Guilford.

Sedikides, C., Wildschut, T., Arndt, J., and Routledge, C. (2008). Nostalgia: Past, present, and future. *Current Directions in Psychological Science, 17,* 304-307.

Seligman, M. E. P. (1975). *Helplessness: On depression, development, and death.* San Francisco: Freeman

Sherman, D. A. K., Nelson, L. D., and Steele, C. M. (2000). Do messages about health risks threaten the self? Increasing the acceptance of threatening health messages via self-affrmation. *Personality and Social Psychology Bulletin, 26,* 1046–105.

Solomon, S., Greenberg, J., and Pyszczynski, T. (1991). A terror management theory of social behavior: The psychological functions of self-esteem and cultural worldviews. In M. P. Zanna (Ed.), *Advances in Experimental Social Psychology* (Vol. 24, pp. 93-159). New York: Academic Press.

Steele, C. M. (1988). The psychology of self-affirmation: Sustaining the integrity of the self. In L. Berkowitz (Ed.), *Advances in experimental social psychology* (Vol. 21, pp. 261-302). San Diego, CA: Academic Press.

Steele, C. M., and Liu, T. J. (1983). Dissonance processes as self-affirmation. *Journal of Personality and Social Psychology, 45,* 5-19.

Stone, J., Wiegand, A. W., Cooper, J., and Aronson, E. (1997). When exemplification fails: Hypocrisy and the motive for self-integrity. *Journal of Personality and Social Psychology, 72,* 54-65.

Tajfel, H. (Ed.). (1978). *Differentiation between social groups: Studies in the social psychology of intergroup relations.* London: Academic Press.

Taylor, S. E. and Brown, J. D. (1988). Illusion and well-being: A social psychological perspective on mental health. *Psychological Bulletin, 103,* 193-210.

Tesser, A., Crepaz, N., Collins, J. C., Cornell, D., and Beach, S. R. H. (2000). Confluence of self defense mechanisms: On integrating the self zoo. *Personality and Social Psychology Bulletin, 26*, 1476-1489.

Thibaut, J. W., and Kelley, H. H. (1959). *The social psychology of groups.* New York: Wiley.

Thibaut, J. W., and Walker, L. (1975). *Procedural justice: A psychological analysis.* Hillsdale, NJ: Erlbaum.

Triandis, H. C. (1995). *Individualism and collectivism.* Boulder, CO: Westview Press.

Tulving, E. (1985). Memory and consciousness. *Canadian Psychologist, 25*, 1-12.

Tyler, T. R. (1989). The psychology of procedural justice: A test of the group-value model. *Journal of Personality and Social Psychology, 57*, 830-838.

Tyler, T. R. (2000). Social justice: Outcome and procedure. *International Journal of Psychology, 35*, 117-125.

Tyler, T. R., and Blader, S. L. (2000). *Cooperation in groups: Procedural justice, social identity, and behavioral engagement.* Philadelphia: Psychology Press.

Tyler, T. R., and Degoey, P. (1995). Collective restraint in social dilemmas: Procedural justice and social identification effects on support for authorities. *Journal of Personality and Social Psychology, 69*, 482-497.

Tyler, T. R., Degoey, P., and Smith, H. (1996). Understanding why the justice of group procedures matters: A test of the psychological dynamics of the group-value model. *Journal of Personality and Social Psychology, 70*, 913-930.

Van den Bos, K. (2005). What is responsible for the fair process effect? In J. Greenberg and J. A. Colquitt (Eds.), *Handbook of organizational justice* (pp. 273-300). Mahwah, NJ: Lawrence Earlbaum.

Van den Bos, K., Lind, E. A., and Wilke, H. A. M. (2001). The psychology of procedural and distributive justice viewed from the perspective of fairness heuristic theory. In R. Cropanzano (Ed.), *Justice in the workplace: From theory to practice* (Vol. 2, pp. 49-66). Mahwah, NJ: Lawrence Erlbaum.

Van den Bos, K., Lind, E., Vermunt, R., and Wilke, H. A. M. (1997). How do I judge my outcome when I do not know the outcome of others? The psychology of the fair process effect. *Journal of Personality and Social Psychology, 72*, 1034-1046.

Weiner, J., and Brehm, J. W. (1966). Buying behavior as a function of verbal and monetary inducements. In J. W. Brehm (Ed.), *A theory of psychological reactance* (pp. 82–90). New York: Academic Press.

Wildschut, T., Sedikides, C., Arndt, J., and Routledge, C. (2006). Nostalgia: Content, triggers, functions. *Journal of Personality and Social Psychology, 91*, 975-993.

Wortman, C.B. and Brehm, J.W. (1975). Response to uncontrollable outcomes: An integration of reactance theory and the learned helplessness model. In L. Berkowitz, (ed.), *Advances in experimental social psychology*, Vol. 8. New York: Academic Press.

Zadro, L., Williams, K. D., and Richardson, R. (2004). How low can you go? Exclusion by a computer is sufficient to lower self-reported levels of belonging, control, self-esteem, and meaningful existence. *Journal of Experimental Social Psychology,* 40, 560-567.

In: Psychology of Threat   ISBN: 978-1-62257-344-8
Editors: B. Hunter and T. Romero   © 2013 Nova Science Publishers, Inc.

Chapter 2

ATTENTION PROCESSES FOR THREATENING HEALTH INFORMATION - A NEUROSCIENTIFIC APPROACH

Loes T. E. Kessels and Robert A. C. Ruiter

Department of Work and Social Psychology,
Maastricht University, The Netherlands

Abstract

Threatening health information has the goal to encourage and motivate people to engage in health promoting and disease preventive behaviours and thus reduce health problems and costs in our society. Evidence shows however that threatening health information often fails to bring about a successful behavioural change. Although the frequently used method of health threat information is assumed to lead to more systematic processing of information containing recommended actions, empirical findings have detected defensive responses towards the health threat information itself, especially among those for whom the health threat is high as opposed to low self-relevant. The present chapter provides insights in the ways people process (self-relevant) threatening health information by studying attention allocation processes during message exposure. Measuring attention processes for health education messages is crucial because attention for the health message is a prerequisite for effective health education. We used measures of EEG, eye movements and reaction times to measure attention processes non-invasively and objectively during message processing. In three empirical studies that will be reported and discussed supported the hypothesis that threatening health information can cause defensive reactions, especially when the information is self-relevant. The integration of neuroscience in health psychology led to a more complete understanding of the underlying attention processes for threatening health information by providing evidence that defensive responses are already present in the very early stages of information processing, at the basic level of attention allocation. It is concluded that communicating self-relevant information and coping information, instead of threatening health information, are promising strategies to increase attention from the reader for the health information.

Introduction

Health education messages have the goal to encourage and motivate people to engage in health promoting and disease preventive behaviours and thus reduce health problems and costs in our society. Evidence shows however that health messages often fail to bring about a successful behavioural change (Parrott, 1995). Changing people's health-related behaviour is a difficult and complex task (Joffe, 2000; Lawrence, 1999; Norton, 1998; Whitehead and Russell, 2004). Partly, this failure can be attributed to the ways that people process the information they have been exposed to (Levy and Windahl, 1985).

The goal of health education practitioners is to create health education messages that result in attitude changes that are stable and predictive of behaviour and more resistant to counterarguments. A prerequisite for achieving this goal is that people attend to the persuasive message to which they are exposed to (Blumberg, 2000; McGuire, 1985). One frequently used health education method that has been assumed to increase message attention is the presentation of threatening health information, presumably because negative information is believed to attract more attention than positive information (see also Baron, Logan, Lilly, Inman, and Brennan, 1994, Baumeister, Bratslavsky, Finkenauer, and Vohs, 2001; Smith, Cacioppo, Larsen, and Chartrand, 2003; Taylor, 1991). However, a large body of experimental research suggests that people who are at risk report the least motivation to change and subsequently react defensively to threatening health information (e.g., Brown and Locker, 2009; Croyle, Sun, and Hart, 1997; Ditto and Croyle, 1995; Freeman, Hennessy, and Marzullo, 2001; Keller, 1999; Keller and Block, 1999; Liberman and Chaiken, 1992).

The focus of this chapter is to answer the important question whether threat information leads to more message involvement and thus more systematic processing of the persuasive information or leads to less message involvement and more defensive reaction, especially among those for whom the information is self-relevant. We will start with a general outline of threatening health information as a behavior change method after which possible defensive mechanisms for threatening health information will be explained in more detail. Then, neuroscience studies will be discussed that investigate attention processes for nutrition and anti-smoking information varying in levels of relevance and threat. The chapter will conclude with recommendations for health education materials and future research suggestions.

Threatening Health Information

In health education threatening health information is used to arouse fear in order to promote precautionary motivation and self-protective action such as not smoking, using seat belts and having a healthy diet (Rogers, 1983). A recent example is the advice of the European Union Commission for Health and Consumer Protection to the EU member states to add shocking graphic pictures to existing health warnings on cigarette packages. These pictures include hard-hitting photographs of, for example, rotten lungs and an open tumor on the throat that should motivate smokers to quit smoking.

Several theoretical models have been formulated to explain the effects of threatening health messages on persuasion. The Parallel Response Model (PRM; Leventhal, 1970), for example, emphasized on the cognitive antecedents of self-protective action. The PRM suggest that threatening health messages cause distinct motivational and coping responses, particularly fear control and danger control. Fear control entails emotion-focused coping (Lazarus and Folkman, 1984), that generates reassurance through denial of the threat or derogation of the message (Ruiter, Abraham, and Kok, 2001). Fear control attempts to control fear generated by the threat and is thus maladaptive because it does not avert the perceived threat (Leventhal, 1971; Witte, 1992). Danger control can be thought of as a cognitive evaluation process orientated towards the presented threat rather than the evoked fear, to stimulate protective action. Danger control thus attempts to control the presented threat. Although fear control and danger control processes are thought to operate independently one may dominate the other (Leventhal, 1970, 1971). According to PRM, fear arousal should precede the danger control processes that underpin precautionary motivation. On the other hand, fear can also activate emotion-focussed processes that may reduce precautionary motivation (Leventhal, 1971; Ruiter et al., 2001).

Leventhal's PRM was further elaborated by Rogers resulting in the Protection Motivation Theory (PMT; Rogers, 1975). According to PMT, danger control in reaction to threatening health messages constitutes two mediating cognitive processes: threat appraisal and coping appraisal. Threat appraisal consists of evaluations of threat seriousness and personal susceptibility (i.e., severity and susceptibility). Coping appraisal consists of evaluations of the effectiveness of potential responses and one's ability to undertake these successfully (i.e, response efficacy and self-efficacy). Threat and coping appraisal generate protection motivation defined as "an intervening variable that has the typical characteristics of a motive: it arouses, sustains, and directs activity" (Rogers, 1975, p. 98).

According to PRM and PMT the chance of accepting the recommendation is more likely when threat increases, but only if the recommendation is judged to be an effective and feasible way to reduce the threat. Individuals will not take protective actions that are supposed to be ineffective in averting the negative consequences. PMT, for example, suggests that the motivation to act will rise when becoming conscious of the severity of a threat that one is susceptible to but that the nature of this motivation is dependent on coping appraisal (i.e., response efficacy and self-efficacy). If the recommended protective action is seen as ineffective in preventing the threat or people feel unable to carry out the recommended action then people will have no intention to act. In the organization of threatening health messages, subdivided in threat information and coping information, coping beliefs thus have a large influence on subsequent health promoting behaviour (Abraham, Sheeran, Abrams, and Spears, 1994; Rippetoe and Rogers, 1987; Witte, Berkowitz, Cameron, and McKeon, 1998). In other words, the presentation of threat information alone is not sufficient for stimulating adaptive action; a positive coping appraisal process is required to motivate people to change risk behaviour and adopt safer behavioural alternatives (Abraham et al., 1994; Rippetoe and Rogers, 1987; Witte et al., 1998). Therefore, an effective threatening persuasive message comprises of threat information that describes the *severity* of the threat and the person's *susceptibility* to it (e.g., "Lung cancer is a deadly disease and those who smoke may acquire it"), accompanied by coping information outlining the *feasibility* and *effectiveness* of a recommended action (e.g., "Quitting smoking may help you in preventing lung cancer").

Combining PRM and PMT, Witte proposed the extended parallel process model (EPPM; Witte, 1992). The EPPM explains both successes and failures of fear appeals through incorporating both fear control and danger control processes. When perceiving threat, danger control processes will initially be activated. Recommended actions will be judged on their effectiveness and feasibility. Judging the response as effective and feasible will motivate the recipient to undertake the recommended action. Judging the recommended action as ineffective or impossible however will lead to negative emotions and fear arousal in particular if threat perception continues. At this moment, fear control processes are instigated leading to denial and avoidance coping. According to EPPM, threat perceptions thus contributes to the extent of a response to a fear appeal (i.e., how strong the danger or fear control responses are), whereas perceived efficacy (or lack thereof) contributes to the nature of the response (whether danger of fear control responses are elicited; Witte, 1992).

Consistent with these assumptions, a meta-analysis (Milne, Sheeran, and Orbell, 2000) indicated that threat appraisal (i.e., severity and susceptibility) and response efficacy measures, have small associations with concurrent behaviour, and do not predict future behaviour. Self-efficacy on the other hand is a strong predictor of concurrent and future behaviour. In line with the larger domain of attitude-behaviour research, efficacy components are stronger determinants of protective action than threat perceptions (see also Floyd, Prentice-Dunn, and Rogers, 2000; Godin and Kok, 1996). For the creation of threatening health messages, presenting coping information is thus important because it can enhance self-efficacy (Moriarty and Stryker, 2008).

Besides the theoretical social cognitive models, interpretations of the impact of fear appeals are also explained by dual-process models of persuasion. While the social cognitive models of threatening health messages were explicitly developed to explain the role of fear arousal in persuasion, the dual-process models like the elaboration likelihood model (ELM) and the heuristic systematic model (HSM), explain the role of any factor in persuasion. The ELM and HSM suggest that threat perception and fear arousal will increase the relevance of threat-relevant information, and, therefore, result in systematic processing of threat-relevant persuasive information (Das, de Wit, and Stroebe, 2003; Ruiter, Abraham et al., 2001). The increased message involvement leading to systematic processing will initiate attitude changes that are more stable and predictive of behaviour and more resistant to counterargumentation (Baron et al., 1994; Chaicken and Trope, 1999; Eagly and Chaicken, 1993). For example, Das and colleagues (2003) hypothesized that inducing vulnerability to a severe health threat communication will cause biased and systematic processing of the action recommendation or coping. Individuals who are vulnerable to a health risk will attempt to make the recommendation appear highly effective by means of a biased search for arguments supporting the effectiveness of the protective action and through biased evaluation of these arguments (Das et al., 2003). The results provided support for their hypotheses, with high-vulnerability participants reporting more thoughts and also more positive (but not negative) thoughts about the recommended action, suggesting increases rather than decreases in the depth of processing and a biased evaluation of the evidences presented (Das et al., 2003).

Defensive Processing of Threatening Information

The above theoretical frameworks suggest that fear appeals, including high threat information and positive coping information, can lead to more adaptive behaviour change. Although threat information is assumed to lead to more systematic but biased processing of information containing recommended actions, empirical findings have also detected defensive responses towards the threat information itself. A considerable body of experimental studies suggest a negative effect of threatening health information on message acceptance, especially among those for whom the health threat is high as opposed to low self-relevant (Brown and Locker, 2009; Croyle et al., 1997; Ditto and Croyle, 1995; Freeman et al., 2001; Harris and Napper, 2005; Keller, 1999; Keller and Block, 1999; Liberman and Chaiken, 1992; Sherman, Nelson, and Steele, 2000; Taubman - Ben-Ari, Florian, and Mikulincer, 2000).

For example, Liberman and Chaicken (1992) presented coffee-drinking and non-coffee drinking participants with threatening information linking coffee-drinking to the development of fibrocystic disease (a precursor of breast cancer). The findings based on self-report questionnaires showed that women coffee-drinkers, for whom the message was highly relevant, were less persuaded of the link between caffeine and fibrocystic disease than female non-coffee drinkers. More importantly, coffee-drinkers seemed to have systematically processed the threatening parts of the message, in a defensive, biased manner. Compared with non-coffee drinkers, they were less critical of information supporting the link. Thus, people for whom the health message had high self-relevance seemed to process the threat information more defensively than people who already followed the recommendations.

Also Keller (1999, Experiment 1) in the context of AIDS prevention research, provided evidence that fear appeals seem to be least effective for those that are most at risk. Among the participants who used a condom whenever they engaged in vaginal sex in the past six months, those who were exposed to a moderate fear message about the health consequences of unsafe sex (e.g., AIDS related cancers, syphilis, death) had more positive intentions to use a condom and showed less message discounting than those who received a low fear-arousing message. In contrast, among those who did not have consistently safe sex during the past six months the low rather than the moderate fear message resulted in more persuasion and less message discounting, again based on questionnaires. Freeman and colleagues (2001) replicated Keller's (1999) finding that fear-arousing persuasive messages seem to be less effective for those who perform risky behaviours. They exposed regular smokers to anti-smoking videos and found that they evaluated the video contents as less effective than non-smokers.

Empirical findings thus support the hypothesis that self-relevant health messages are received with more defensive reaction to the extent that they more vividly present the negative consequences of risky health behaviour. Sherman and colleagues (2000) hypothesized that this defensive motivation stems from the anticipation that threatening information will damage the self-image. Two experimental studies suggested that defensive processing may help to maintain a positive self-image. Among respondents for whom the presented threat was highly relevant, those who maintained a positive self-image through self-affirmation techniques were less defensive and more accepting of health information than those whose central values were not affirmed (Harris, Mayle, Mabbott, and Napper, 2007; Harris and Napper, 2005; Sherman et al., 2000; Van Koningsbruggen and Das, 2009; Van Koningsbruggen, Das, and Roskos-Ewoldsen, 2009). Theoretically, these findings can be explained in cognitive dissonance theory (Festinger, 1957) and Kunda's (1990) argument for motivated reasoning: Individuals experiencing dissonance because their self-image is threatened (e.g., smokers exposed to threatening health commercials about smoking) are motivated to reduce it by changing one of the implicated cognitive or behavioural elements, for example through biased processing of presented information (e.g., Liberman and Chaiken, 1992) or message derogation (e.g., Keller, 1999).

Overall, based on self-report measures and measures of response times and reading times it has been concluded that people for whom the health message had high self-relevance seemed to process the threat information more defensively than people who already followed the recommendations (see also Harris et al., 2007; Harris and Napper, 2005; Noar, Benac, and Harris, 2007; Sherman et al., 2000).

In the light of these defensive results, the important question arises whether threat information leads to more message involvement and thus more systematic processing of the persuasive information as was assumed by the presented models or leads to less message involvement and more defensive reactions, especially among those for whom the information is self-relevant.

Understanding Underlying Processes

Although fear appeals assume more message involvement and thus heightened attention for the health threat information (Baron et al., 1994; Brug, Oenema, and Campbell, 2003; Kreuter and Holt, 2001), the few studies that investigated underlying working mechanisms showed contrasting results. Fear appeals can cause defensive reactions among those for whom the information is most self-relevant. Although these studies tried to investigate whether the presented information caused more systematic processing, thus assuming more attention allocated to the health message, the direct effects of health message on processes of attention allocation have not been studied systematically yet.

Measuring attention processes for health education messages is crucial because attention for the information is a prerequisite for effective health education (Blumberg, 2000; McGuire, 1985). McGuire's (1985) persuasion-communication model states that people should first be exposed to the stimulus message and then attend to it, followed by accurate comprehension of the presented information and integration of new information with previous knowledge to arrive at an attitudinal judgment. According to this model, a prerequisite for effective health education is that people allocate sufficient attention resources to the persuasive message they are exposed to (Blumberg, 2000; McGuire, 1985). Health messages can thus already fail in the early process of message attention. Remarkably, persuasion research has largely ignored attention as a dependent variable in evaluation studies.

The few studies investigating attention processes for health education messages were limited to indirect measures of attention. For example, self-report measures of cognitive effort (Liberman and Chaiken, 1992) and more implicit measures of reading time (Brown and Locker, 2009) and response time (Klein and Harris, 2009) have been used to provide an index of the amount of attention that was allocated to threatening health information. However, by definition these measures do not allow a direct observation of the amount of attention that is allocated to the threatening information *during* message processing. At best, the procedures reflect relatively late information processing stages that feed higher order cognitive processes such as biased processing and not the early stage of attention allocation.

A major limitation of self-report measures is that they require introspection from the participants while people may not be aware of motives that drive their behaviour (Wilson, 2002; Wilson and Dunn, 2004). Furthermore, participants may respond with social desirable statements. With regard to the earlier mentioned warning messages on tobacco packages, Ruiter and Kok (2005) argued that campaign effects of fear arousal on smoking behaviour based on self-reports are not consistent with objectively measured effects. People are full of good intention, especially when being confronted with significant health threats, but seldom act towards these intentions. Caution should be used when interpreting self-report measures. From a scientific point of view, but also a practical point of view, it is important to identify the conditions that determine whether people attend to health messages or not. Therefore, we investigated early attention processes when people are exposed to the persuasive method of threatening health information in a more objective way through using the techniques of electroencephalogram (EEG) to record electrical brain activity, eye tracking and reaction times (RT). No previous research has investigated the effects of (self-relevant) threatening health information on processes of attention allocation during message processing.

EEG

In three studies attention processes were examined by using the method of measuring electroencephalogram (EEG) to record electrical brain activity (Kessels, Ruiter, Brug, and Jansma, 2011; Kessels, Ruiter, and Jansma, 2010; Ruiter, Kessels, Jansma, and Brug, 2006). A primary motivation to use EEG is the excellent (millisecond) temporal resolution resulting in measures of the time course of cognitive processes with great precision. From the continuous measure of brain activity (EEG) event-related potentials (ERPs) are generated. ERPs are the electric potentials that are specifically time locked to an internal or external event. By measuring ERPs the chronology of mental processes can be linked to the neural activations occurring after a sensory stimulus (Srinivasan, 2004). An ERP component that is of special interest in our studies is the P300. The P300 refers to a positive peak with a modal latency of 300 msec (Fabiani, Gratton, and Coles, 2000) and is strongly influenced by the task demands that are laid on the participants. The P300, frequently measured in attention paradigms, is functionally related to late conscious, decisional and premotor response related stages. The P300 which is usually strongest at central-parietal scalp sites, reflects relatively late and more controlled attention processes and as such provides an index for a cognitively driven allocation of attention and an update of stimulus processing with working memory information (e.g., Coull, 1998; Hillyard, Mangun, Woldorff, and Luck, 1995; Näätänen, 1992). The P300 is typically elicited by novel and low probability (rare) stimuli, but is also sensitive to other parameters such as task relevance.

Message Tailoring - Nutrition Information

The aim of our first two studies was to investigate underlying working mechanisms of self-relevant threatening nutrition information during message exposure through using the techniques of EEG and reaction times (Kessels et al., 2011; Ruiter et al., 2006). Previous research suggest that self-relevance heightens attention for the information, but only if this information is non-threatening. When the information contains high threat information, less attention will be paid to the self-relevant health information. In a first study we investigated if self-relevant information heightens attention for nutrition information (Ruiter et al., 2006). In a second study we combined self-relevant information and threat information to investigate if self-relevant threatening nutrition information causes defensive responses, reflected in less attention for the nutrition information (Kessels et al., 2011).

We explored attention processes for self-relevant information through using the persuasive method of message tailoring (Ruiter et al., 2006). Message tailoring can be defined as any combination of information or change strategies intended to reach one specific person, based on characteristics that are unique to that person, related to the outcome of interest, and have been derived from an individual assessment (Kreuter, Bull, Clark, and Oswald, 1999; Kreuter, Farrell, Olevitch, and Brennan, 2000). A message is thus created that closely responds to the needs of the targeted individual based on an earlier individual assessment. Evidence shows that message tailoring is associated with better behaviour change effects than generic health education, especially in nutrition education interventions (Brug et al., 2003; Kreuter, et al., 2000; Kroeze, Werkman, and Brug, 2006; Noar et al., 2007; Rimer and Glassman, 1999; Skinner, Campbell, Rimer, Curry, and Prochaska, 1999). Research in the Netherlands showed that computer-tailored nutrition interventions resulted in a 5.4 % lower fat intake, compared with a 1.4% drop in a general nutrition information control group (Brug et al., 2003).

In a dual-processing task, participants were reading nutrition education messages and at the same time attention had to be paid to specific odd auditory stimuli in a sequence of frequent auditory stimuli (odd ball paradigm). The amount of attention allocation was measured by recording event-related brain potentials (ERPs) and reaction times (RT) to the auditory task. We assumed that the observed auditory attention effects in the ERPs and reaction times could be used as an inverted index of the amount of perceptual and cognitive attention resources allocated to the reading of the nutrition advice. Due to limited attention resources it was hypothesized that there should be more auditory attention paid to the target tones during the reading of the non-tailored nutrition advice than during the reading of the tailored nutrition advice.

As predicted, the observed P300 attention effects at central-parietal sites, which reflect attention allocation to the auditory task in a relatively late stage of information processing (i.e., at the interface between sensory and memory processing), were higher for the participants who read the non-tailored nutrition advice than for those who read the tailored advice. Based on the assumption of resource allocation (Kok, 1997; Sanders, 1997), these modulations of the P300 effect thus suggest that the tailored information received more attention from the participants than the non-tailored information. Support for our hypothesis was also observed in the reaction time data. Although the reaction times did not significantly differ between participants in the tailored intervention group and those in the non-tailored intervention group, the means were in the predicted direction (faster for non-tailored compared to tailored group – presumably due to attention allocation) and a medium to large effect size (Cohen, 1998) was reported.

In sum, the data give additional and methodological new empirical evidence on previous explanations of the positive effects of computer-tailored health information that referred to the relative gain in attention for individualized health information, but were only indirectly supported by self-report measures that *followed* exposure to the stimulus information (e.g., Brug, Glanz, Van Assema, Kok, and Van Breukelen, 1998). These findings provide support for the dual process models of attitude change that hold that self-relevant information is more systematically processed than information that is less self-relevant (e.g., Petty and Cacioppo, 1986).

In our second ERP study tailored nutrition health information was combined with either high or low threatening health information (Kessels et al., 2011). Tailored and non-tailored nutrition education messages were presented. Both messages were supplemented with high threat or low threat nutrition information in order to investigate the effects of self-relevant nutrition information, through message tailoring, in combination with health threat information on attention allocation processes. Attention effects on the combination of message tailoring and threatening health information were investigated by using the same oddball paradigm as in the first ERP study.

Besides a replication of our first ERP study, showing positive attention effects for message tailoring, the results showed also more attention for low threat information compared with high threat information. In addition to the first ERP study, attention enhancement for tailored information was also found on the reaction time data. This suggests that not only at the beginning, but also at the end of the cognitive process (during motor preparation) attention is modulated by message relevance.

Interestingly, the results on the self-report measure of perceived attention did not support the results on the ERP and the reaction times data in both studies. Both ERP studies showed no significant differences between the two tailoring conditions in subjective estimates of the extent to which respondents read the information carefully. These findings implicate the usefulness of more objective measures (e.g., ERPs) when studying important psychological processes underlying the effectiveness of health communications. Although participants might not consciously experience their relative attention gain for certain information, measures of ERPs and reaction times are able to surface these positive effects in an objective way.

Anti-Smoking Materials

Threatening health information is also frequently applied in anti-smoking health materials. Nowadays, most cigarette packages include health warning labels (e.g., "Smoking causes fatal lung cancer") and/or pictures (e.g., black lungs) with the aim to motivate people to refrain from smoking. A large body of self-report studies suggest that health warning labels on cigarette packages are effective in informing people about the negative health consequences of smoking (Bansal-Travers, Hammond, Smith, and Cummings, 2011; de Hoog, Stroebe, and De Wit, 2007; deTurck, Rachlin, and Young, 1994; Fong, Hammond, Jiang, Li, Quah, Driezen, and Yan, 2010; Hammond, 2011; Hammond, Fong, McNeill, Borland, and Cummings, 2006; Nascimento, et al., 2008; Thrasher, Rousu, Hammond, Navarro, and Corrigan, 2011; Thrasher, Rousu, Anaya-Ocampo, Reynales-Shigematsu, Arillo-Santillán, and Hernández-Ávila, 2007). The self-reported cognitive and behavioural impact of health warning labels was found to be largest with prominent labels (i.e., in front and back of the package) supplemented with emotionally graphic warnings that demonstrate the negative bodily impacts or human suffering due to smoking (Bansal-Travers et al., 2011; Fong et al., 2010; Thrasher, et al., 2011; Thrasher, Villalobos, Szklo, Fong, Pérez, and Sebrié, 2010). Research on appraisal, recall and level of engagement showed the largest impact when anti-tobacco television ads were presented with 'visceral negative' themes (Terry-McElrath, Wakefield, Ruel, Balch, Emery, Szczypka, Clegg-Smith, and Flay, 2005). Particularly for starters and smokers intending to quit smoking, graphic warnings that are highly visible and show the negative health consequences of smoking were identified as successful vehicles for reducing smoking prevalence (Hammond et al., 2006).

However, most studies into the effectiveness of graphic cigarette health warnings rely on self-report measures. This runs the risk of false introspection from the participants as people may not be aware of (implicit) motives that drive their behaviour (Falk, 2010; Harris et al., 2007; Ruiter and Kok, 2005; Ruiter and

Kok, 2006). Self-report measures of cognitive effort (Liberman and Chaicken, 1992) and more implicit measures of reading time (Brown and Locker, 2009) and response time (Klein and Harris, 2009) have been used to provide an index of the amount of attention that is allocated to threatening health information. As was already pointed out, these studies suggest that people most at risk react defensively to threatening health information by attending away from the message (or by avoiding the message). No previous studies measured direct attention processes for cigarette health warnings among people for whom the information is self-relevant (i.e. smokers) or non self-relevant (i.e., non-smokers).

We explored specific covert attention capture and holding processes for high and low threatening smoking pictures among smokers and non-smokers (Kessels et al., 2010). In the visual attention system a distinction can be made between attention capture and attention holding processes. Automatic attention capture is usually driven by salient characteristics of the stimuli (for example its valence). The visual attention system also decides whether the stimulus needs to hold attention or whether it is important to shift the attention focus to another place, i.e. attention disengagement (Posner, Walker, Friedrich, and Rafal, 1984). For example, Koster, Crombez, Van Damme, Verschuere, and De Houwer (2004) provided evidence that imminent threat causes attention capture and attention holding, caused by the phylogenetically old mechanism that directs attention to imminent threat automatically. In the present study we hypothesized that although threatening health information will automatically causes attention capture because of its obvious survival value, it will also motivate people to reduce their feeling of dissonance when the information undermines self-relevant goals by disengaging attention from it. People for whom the threat information is self-relevant will thus be motivated to avoid this information by disengaging from the threat. The latter is, for example, reflected in the use of less cognitive resources in detecting visual targets presented in other areas of the visual scene than the threatening cue.

In a variant of the Posner cueing task (1980), ERPs and reaction times were measured for self-relevant smoking threat information. Participants reacted to a *target* (two horizontal or two vertical dots) presented at the left or right visual field. This target was preceded by a *cue* (i.e., high and low threat smoking pictures) at either the target location (valid trials; 82%) or at the opposite location (invalid trials; 18%). In invalid trials, reflecting attention disengagement processes, attention must be disengaged from the incorrect location and has to be reallocated towards the target position. We expected that people react defensively to self-relevant threatening health information by disengaging from it. In other words, smokers will more easily disengage attention from high threat smoking pictures than will those less affected by the health threat (non-smokers).

Our ERP findings for the smoking participants are in line with the view that people are motivated to reduce feelings of cognitive dissonance (Festinger, 1957; Kunda, 1990). While previous studies used self-report measures or implicit measures of reading time and response time, the present study provided evidence for motivated reasoning through the use of attention measures during message processing (Brown and Locker, 2009; Klein and Harris, 2009). The ERP findings showed that smokers disengaged more efficiently from high threat as opposed to low threat health information, implicating that people whose self-image was threatened tried to avoid the high threat information. The ERP findings thus indicate that avoidance responses can already arise at the early process of attention allocation.

Besides our specific attention disengagement hypothesis we predicted, based on the attention preference mechanism for imminent threat, more attention capture for high as opposed to low threat pictures for both smokers and non-smokers (Koster, Crombez, Van Damme et al., 2004). Support for our hypothesis was observed in the parietal distributed P300 amplitudes in reaction to the valid targets, with higher amplitudes for the high threat than for the low threat trials. This finding indicates that both smokers and non-smokers used increased resources to capture attention for high threat smoking information irrespective of whether the information was self-relevant or not.

Among smokers, the ERP results showed more efficient disengagement processes for high threat compared to low threat smoking pictures. Furthermore, both smokers and non-smokers revealed more attention capture processes for high threat compared to low threat smoking pictures. When measuring covert attention processes two different patterns of results were detected. First, threatening health information automatically captures attention irrespective of the self-relevance of the information. Second, threatening health information causes more efficient attention disengagement when the information is self-relevant. The present findings indicate that whether high threat health information attracts and holds attention is dependent upon whether the information is self-relevant or not. In line with previous research, indicating that high threat health information causes denial as a coping strategy (Brown and Locker, 2009), the use of high threat information may be counterproductive for people performing the risky behaviour.

Coping Information

Leading theoretical frameworks on the use of threatening health messages, such as protection motivation theory (Rogers, 1975) and the extended parallel process model (Witte, 1992), dictate that for threatening health messages to be effective individuals must feel capable to perform the recommended action (i.e., high self-efficacy, Bandura, 1997). For a range of health-related behaviours, self-efficacy beliefs have been identified as strong determinants of behaviour change and maintenance (Bandura, 1986; de Vries and Backbier, 1994; Forsyth and Carey, 1998; Godin and Kok, 1996; Maibach and Murphy, 1995). In addition, meta-analyses of fear appeal studies have identified self-efficacy and not risk perception as a major predictor of the intention to undertake action to protect health (de Vries and Backbier, 1994; Floyd et al., 2000; Godin and Kok, 1996; Maibach and Murphy, 1995; Milne et al., 2000; Witte and Allen, 2000). While self-efficacy is one of the most widely applied constructs across theories of health behaviour and presenting information that provides help to undertake action to protect health (i.e., coping information) might increase levels of self-efficacy (Woodgate and Brawley, 2008), coping information is only rarely presented in health messages in the public domain (Moriarty and Stryker, 2008). For example, only 2 of the 14 recently introduced graphic warnings labels on cigarette packages in the European Community provide information that might aid smokers with translating intention to quit smoking into quitting behaviour ('Your doctor or pharmacist can help you stop smoking' and 'get help to stop smoking: 0803000000'). To take action, individuals need to know what to do and have to believe that they are capable to perform the action (Bandura, 1997) and presenting coping information might increase levels of self-efficacy (Woodgate and Brawley, 2008).

The primary purpose of our last study was to examine the amount of attention allocation to threat and coping information on cigarette packages (Kessels and Ruiter, submitted for publication). Sixteen self-created cigarette packages were created containing health texts that presented either high risk or coping information combined with a high threat or a low threat smoking-related photo. We chose to use the method of eye-movement registration to measure attention allocation processes for the packages. Eye-movement registration enables us to measure the course of attention over longer periods of time (Thomsen and Fulton, 2007). Evidence was sought for the hypothesis that people for whom the health risk text is self-relevant (i.e., smokers) will react defensively to this information by spending less attention – reflected in fewer fixations and less dwell time – to high risk as opposed to coping text. For non-smokers, we expect that high risk information might attract more automatic attention than coping information because of the evolutionary value to detect risks (e.g. predator) over benefits (e.g., food; Koster, Crombez, Van Damme, et al., 2004; Mogg and Bradley, 1998).

Results of the eye movement data showed that smokers tend to spend more time looking (i.e., more unique fixations and longer dwell time) at the coping information than at the high risk information irrespective of the content of the smoking-related photo. Non-smokers tend to spend more time looking at the high risk information than at the coping information when the information was presented in combination with a high threat smoking photo. When a low threat photo was presented, non-smokers paid more attention to the coping information than to the high risk information. Results for the smoking photos showed more attention allocation for low threat photos that were presented in combination with high risk information than for low threat photos in combination with coping information. No attention differences were found for the high threat photos.

By recording eye movements, we concluded that written coping information presented on cigarette packages attracts more attention from the viewer than high risk textual information, especially for those for whom the information is self-relevant (i.e., smokers). For non-smokers, for whom the health information is not self-relevant findings show mixed results, with attention preferences for coping information only when the information is combined with a low threat photo. This finding is in line with meta-analysis studies into the effectives of behavioural change interventions in other health domains such as HIV/AIDS and nutrition and physical activity (Albarracín, Gillette, Earl, Glasman, Durantini, and Ho, 2005; Michie, Abraham, Whittington, McAteer, and Gupta, 2009). These studies show that providing instructions about how to effectively adopt healthy behaviour could be a more useful tool in health education message design than providing threat information about the negative consequences of unhealthy behaviour X. The findings of the present study support this conclusion. The preference for coping information is not reflected in current health messages to motivate smokers to quit smoking. Coping information should be more frequently implemented in health message design to increase attention for these messages and thus contribute to effective persuasion.

Conclusion

In this chapter, we described the underlying working mechanisms of threatening health information as a method to induce behaviour change. Based on the attention studies we described in this chapter the following conclusions can be drawn.

We can conclude that message tailoring is a potentially effective tool to increase attention for health information. Message tailoring increases attention for the information. Measuring divided attention processes when using the oddball paradigm showed that people direct more attention to tailored than to non-tailored nutrition education messages (Kessels et al., 2011; Ruiter et al., 2006). Communicating self- relevant information is a promising strategy to increase attention from the reader for the health information.

Investigating the relation between self-relevance, threatening health information and attention reveals a more complex pattern of results. The measure of divided attention processes shows less attention for threatening nutrition health information irrespective of the self-relevance of the information (Kessels et al., 2011). When measuring selective attention processes, through using a cueing paradigm, high threat health information increases attention capture irrespective of the self-relevance of the information (Kessels et al., 2010). However, high threat health information that is self-relevant also induces defensive responses. Participants confronted with self-relevant high threat smoking information showed more efficient disengagement from the information than when receiving non self-relevant high threat information (Kessels et al., 2010). The measure of overt attention processes, through measuring eye movements for cigarette packages, show that written coping information presented on cigarette packages attracts more attention from the viewer than high risk textual information, especially for those for whom the information is self-relevant (i.e., smokers, Kessels and Ruiter, submitted for publication). Providing coping information or self-relevant low threat information instead of high threat information seems preferable to increase attention for persuasive information.

To measure attention processes for health information it is recommended to apply neuroscience techniques to obtain non-invasive and objective measures of attention during message processing. Neuroscience methods can provide information that would be impossible to gather with other techniques such as self-report questionnaires. Social neuroscience is a growing field of research. To get a more complete understanding of human behaviour, psychology needs neuroscience and neuroscience needs psychology (Harmon-Jones and Beer, 2009). Through integrating neuroscience into social psychology we gathered a more complex understanding of attention processes for different health education messages.

Finally, caution when using high threat health information should be taken. Providing high threat health information seems to induce defensive reactions reflected in less attention for the information. Our studies show that it is necessary to thoroughly pretest health communication materials in experimental studies even when some strategies seem obviously more effective or better than others. They may cause unexpected and unwanted side effects. More research on factors that trigger defensive reactions or increase attention for the information and subsequently whether these attention effects lead to behaviour change is desirable and necessary.

In sum, the use of non-invasive measurement techniques (e.g., EEG or eye-tracking) allowed us to measure attention processes during message exposure. The integration of neuroscience in health psychology led to a more complete understanding of the underlying attention processes of different persuasive techniques. Providing tailored health education materials and coping information are strategies that increase attention for health information. Threatening health information can cause defensive responses. Therefore, providing tailored information or providing instructions about how to effectively adopt healthy behaviour could be a more useful tool in health education message design than providing threat information about the negative consequences of unhealthy behaviour X.

References

Abraham, C. S., Sheeran, P., Abrams, D., and Spears, R. (1994). Exploring teenagers' adaptive and maladaptive thinking in relation to the threat of HIV infection. *Psychology and Health, 9*, 253-272.

Albarracín, D., Gillette, J. C., Earl, A. N., Glasman, L. R., Durantini, M. R., and Ho, M.-H. (2005). A test of major assumptions about behavior change: A comprehensive look at the effects of passive and active HIV-prevention interventions since the beginning of the epidemic. *Psychological Bulletin, 131*, 856-897.

Bandura, A. (1986). *Social foundations of thought and action: A social cognitive theory*. Englewood Cliffs, NJ: Prentice-Hall.

Bandura, A. (1997). *Self-efficacy: The exercise of control*. New York: W. H. Freeman.

Bansal-Travers, M., Hammond, D., Smith, P., and Cummings, K. M. (2011). The impact of cigarette pack design, descriptors, and warning labels on risk perception in the U.S. *American Journal of Preventive Medicine, 40*, 674-682.

Baron, R. S., Logan, H., Lilly, J., Inman, M., and Brennan, M. (1994). Negative emotion and message processing. *Social Psychology Quarterly, 30*, 181-201.

Baumeister, R. F., Bratslavsky, E., Finkenauer, C., and Vohs, K. D. (2001). Bad is stronger than good. *Review of General Psychology, 5*, 323-370.

Blumberg, S. J. (2000). Guarding against threatening HIV prevention messages: An information-processing model. *Health Education and Behavior, 27*, 780-795.

Brown, S., and Locker, E. (2009). Defensive responses to an emotive anti-alcohol message. *Psychology and Health,* 24, 517-528.

Brug, J., Glanz, K., Van Assema, P., Kok, G., and Van Breukelen, G. J. P. (1998). The impact of computer-tailored feedback and iterative feedback on fat, fruit, and vegetable intake. *Health Education and Behavior,* 25, 517-531.

Brug, J., Oenema, A., and Campbell, M. K. (2003). Past, present, and future of computer-tailored nutrition education. *American Journal of Clinical Nutrition,* 77, 1028S-1034S.

Chaicken, S., and Trope, Y. (1999). *Dual-process theories in social psychology.* New York: The Guilford Press.

Cohen, J. (1998). *Statisitical power analysis for the behavioral sciences* (2nd ed.). Hillsdale, NJ: Erlbaum.

Coull, J. T. (1998). Neural correlates of attention and arousal: Insights from electrophysiology, functional neuroimaging and psychopharmacology. *Progress in Neurobiology,* 55, 343-361.

Croyle, R. T., Sun, Y., and Hart, M. (1997). Processing risk factor information: Defensive biases in health-related judgments and memory. In K. J. Petrie and J. A. Weinman (Eds.), *Perceptions of health and illness: Current research and applications* (pp. 267-290). Amsterdam: Harwood Academic.

Das, E. H. H. J., de Wit, J. B. F., and Stroebe, W. (2003). Fear appeals motivate acceptance of action recommendations: Evidence for a positive bias in the processing of persuasive messages. *Personality and Social Psychology Bulletin,* 29, 650-664.

de Hoog, N., Stroebe, W., and De Wit, J. (2007). The impact of vulnerability to and severity of a health risk on processing and acceptance of fear-arousing communications: a meta-analysis. *Review of General Psychology,* 11, 258-285.

de Vries, H., and Backbier, E. (1994). Self-efficacy as an important determinant of quitting among pregnant women who smoke: The ø-pattern. *Preventive Medicine: An International Journal Devoted to Practice and Theory,* 23, 167-174.

deTurck, M., Rachlin, R., and Young, M. (1994). Effects of a role-model and fear in warning label on perceptions of safety behavior. *Advances in Consumer Research,* 21, 208-212.

Ditto, P. H., and Croyle, R. T. (1995). Understanding the impact of risk factor test results: Insights from a basic research program. In R. T. Croyle (Ed.), *Psychosocial effects of screening for disease prevention and detection* (pp. 144-181). New York: Oxford University Press.

Eagly, A. H., and Chaicken, S. (1993). *The psychology of attitudes.* Fort Worth, TX: Harcourt Brace Jovanovich.

Fabiani, M., Gratton, G., and Coles, M. G. H. (2000). Event-related brain potentials. In J. T. Cacioppo, L. G. Tassinary and G. G. Berntson (Eds.), *Handbook of psychophysiology* (2nd ed., pp. 53-84). New York: Cambridge University Press.

Falk, E. (2010). Communication neuroscience as a tool for health psychologists. *Health Psychology, 29,* 355-357.

Festinger, L. (1957). *A theory of cognitive dissonance.* Stanford: Stanford University Press.

Floyd, D. L., Prentice-Dunn, S., and Rogers, R. W. (2000). A meta-analysis of research on protection motivation theory. *Journal of Applied Social Psychology,* 30, 407-429.

Fong, G., Hammond, D., Jiang, Y., Li, Q., Quah, A., Driezen, P., and Yan, M. (2010). Perceptions of tobacco health warnings in China compare with picture and text-only health warnings from other countries: an experimental study. *Tobacco Control,* 19, 69-77.

Forsyth, A. D., and Carey, M. P. (1998). Measuring self-efficacy in the context of HIV risk reduction: Research challenges and recommendations. *Health Psychology,* 17, 559-568.

Freeman, M. A., Hennessy, E. V., and Marzullo, D. M. (2001). Defensive evaluation of antismoking messages among college-age smokers: The role of possible selves. *Health Psychology,* 20, 424-433.

Godin, G., and Kok, G. (1996). The theory of planned behavior: A review of its applications to health-related behaviors. *American Journal of Health Promotion,* 11, 87-98.

Hammond, D. (2011). Health warning messages on tobacco products: a review. *Tobacco Control,* 20, 327-337.

Hammond, D., Fong, G., McNeill, A., Borland, R., and Cummings, K. (2006). Effectiveness of cigarette warning labels in informing smokers about the risks of smoking: findings from the International Tobacco Control (ITC) Four Country Survey. *Tobacco Control,* 15, 19-25.

Harmon-Jones, E., and Beer, J. S. (2009). Introduction to social and personality neuroscience methods. In E. Harmon-Jones and J. S. Beer (Eds.), *Methods in social neuroscience* (pp. 1-9). New York: The Guilford Press.

Harris, P. R., Mayle, K., Mabbott, L., and Napper, L. (2007). Self-affirmation reduces smokers' defensiveness to graphic on-pack cigarette warning labels. *Health Psychology,* 26, 437-446.

Harris, P. R., and Napper, L. (2005). Self-Affirmation and the Biased Processing of Threatening Health-Risk Information. *Personality and Social Psychology Bulletin,* 31, 1250-1263.

Hillyard, S. A., Mangun, G. R., Woldorff, M. G., and Luck, S. J. (1995). Neural systems mediating selective attention. In M. S. Gazzaniga (Ed.), *The cognitive neurosciences* (pp. 665-681). Cambridge, MA: MIT Press.

Joffe, H. (2000). Adherence to health messages: A social psychological perspective. *International Dental Journal*, 295-303.

Keller, P. A. (1999). Converting the unconverted: The effect of inclination and opportunity to discount health-related fear appeals. *Journal of Applied Psychology*, 84, 403-415.

Keller, P. A., and Block, L. G. (1999). The effect of affect-based dissonance versus cognition-based dissonance on motivated reasoning and health-related persuasion. *Journal of Experimental Psychology: Applied*, 5, 302-313.

Kessels, L. T. E. and Ruiter, R. A. C. (submitted for publication). Eye movement responses to health messages on cigarette packages.

Kessels, L. T. E., Ruiter, R. A. C., Brug, and Jansma, B. M. (2011). The effects of tailored and threatening nutrition information on message attention. Evidence from an event-related potential study. *Appetite*, 56, 32-38.

Kessels, L. T. E., Ruiter, R. A. C., and Jansma, B. M. (2010). Increased attention but more efficient disengagement: Neuroscientific evidence for defensive processing of threatening health information. *Health Psychology*, 29, 346-354.

Klein, W. M. P., and Harris, P. R. (2009). Self-affirmation enhances attentional bias toward threatening components of a persuasive message. *Psychological Science*, 20, 1463-1467.

Kok, A. (1997). Event-related potential (ERP) reflections of mental resources: A review and synthesis. *Biological Psychology*, 45, 19-56.

Koster, E. H. W., Crombez, G., Van Damme, S., Verschuere, B., and De Houwer, J. (2004). Does Imminent Threat Capture and Hold Attention? *Emotion*, 4, 312-317.

Koster, E. H. W., Crombez, G., Verschuere, B., and De Houwer, J. (2004). Selective attention to threat in the dot probe paradigm: differentiating vigilance and difficulty to disengage. *Behaviour Research and Therapy*, 42, 1183-1192.

Kreuter, M. W., Bull, F. C., Clark, E. M., and Oswald, D. L. (1999). Understanding how people process health information: A comparison of tailored and nontailored weight-loss materials. *Health Psychology*, 18, 487-494.

Kreuter, M. W., Farrell, D., Olevitch, L., and Brennan, M. (2000). *Tailored health messages: Customizing communication with computer technology*. Mahwah, NJ: Lawrence Erlbaum.

Kreuter, M. W., and Holt, C. L. (2001). How do people process health information? Applications in an age of individualized communication. *Current Directions in Psychological Science,* 10, 206-209.

Kroeze, W., Werkman, A., and Brug, J. (2006). A Systematic Review of Randomized Trials on the Effectiveness of Computer-Tailored Education on Physical Activity and Dietary Behaviors. *Annals of Behavioral Medicine,* 31, 205-223.

Kunda, Z. (1990). The case for motivated reasoning. *Psychological Bulletin,* 108, 480-498.

Lawrence, T. (1999). A stage-based approach to behaviour change. In E. R. Perkins, I. Simnett and L. Wright (Eds.), *Evidence-based health promotion* (pp. 64-75). West Sussex, England: Wiley and Sons.

Lazarus, R. S., and Folkman, S. (1984). *Stress, appraisal and coping.* New York: Springer.

Leventhal, H. (1970). Findings and theory in the study of fear communication. In L. Berkowitz (Ed.), *Advances in experimental social psychology* (Vol. 5, pp. 119-186). New York: Academic Press.

Leventhal, H. (1971). Fear appeals and persuasion: The differentiation of a motivational construct. *American Journal of Public Health,* 61, 1208-1224.

Levy, M. R., and Windahl, S. (1985). The concept of audience activity. In K. E. Rosengren, L. A. Wenner and P. Palmgreen (Eds.), *Media gratifications research: Current perspectives* (pp. 109-122). Beverly Hills, CA: Sage.

Liberman, A., and Chaiken, S. (1992). Defensive processing of personally relevant health messages. *Personality and Social Psychology Bulletin, 18,* 669-679.

Maibach, E., and Murphy, D. A. (1995). Self-efficacy in health promotion research and practice: Conceptualization and measurement. *Health Education Research,* 10, 37-50.

McGuire, W. J. (1985). Attitude and attitude change. In G. Lindzey and E. Aronson (Eds.), *The handbook of social psychology* (pp. 233-346). New York: Random House.

Michie, S., Abraham, C., Whittington, C., McAteer, J., and Gupta, S. (2009). Effective techniques in health eating and physical activity interventions: A meta-regression. *Health Psychology,* 28, 690-701.

Milne, S., Sheeran, P., and Orbell, S. (2000). Prediction and intervention in health-related behavior: A meta-analytic review of protection motivation theory. *Journal of Applied Social Psychology,* 30, 106-143.

Mogg, K., Bradley, B. (1998). A cognitive-motivational analysis of anxiety. *Behavioral Research Therapy,* 36, 809-848.

Moriarty, C. M., and Stryker, J. E. (2008). Prevention and screening efficacy messages in newspaper accounts of cancer. *Health Education Research,* 23, 487-498.

Näätänen, R. (1992). *Attention and brain function.* Hillsdale, NJ: Erlbaum.

Nascimento, B. E. M., Oliveira, L., Vieira, A. S., Joffily, M., Gleiser, S., Pereira, M. G., et al., (2008). Avoidance of smoking: The impact of warning labels in Brazil. *Tobacco Control: An International Journal,* 17, 405-409.

Noar, S. M., Benac, C. N., and Harris, M. S. (2007). Does tailoring matter? Meta-analytic review of tailored print health behavior change interventions. *Psychological Bulletin,* 133, 673-693.

Norton, L. (1998). Health promotion and health education: What role should the nurse adopt in practice. *Journal of Advanced Nursing,* 28, 1269-1275.

Parrott, R. L. (1995). Motivation to attend to health messages: Presentation of content and linguistic considerations. In E. Maibach and R. L. Parrott (Eds.), *Designing health messages: Approaches from communication theory and public health practice* (pp. 7-23). Thousand Oaks, CA: Sage.

Petty, R. E., and Cacioppo, J. T. (1986). *Communication and persuasion: Central and peripheral routes to attitude change.* New York: Springer-Verlag.

Posner, M. I., Walker, J. A., Friedrich, F. A., and Rafal, R. D. (1984). Effects of parietal injury on covert orienting of attention. *The Journal of Neuroscience,* 4, 1863-1874.

Rimer, B. K., and Glassman, B. (1999). Is there a use for tailored print communication in cancer risk communication? *Journal of the National Cancer Institute Monographs,* 25, 140-148.

Rippetoe, P. A., and Rogers, R. W. (1987). Effects of components of protection-motivation theory on adaptive and maladaptive coping with a health threat. *Journal of Personality and Social Psychology,* 52, 596-604.

Rogers, R. W. (1975). A protection motivation theory of fear appeals and attitude change. *Journal of Psychology: Interdisciplinary and Applied,* 91, 93-114.

Rogers, R. W. (1983). Cognitive and physiological processes in fear appeals and attitude change: A revised theory of protection motivation. In J. T. Cacioppo and R. E. Petty (Eds.), *Social psychophysiology: A sourcebook* (pp. 153-176). New York: The Guilford Press.

Ruiter, R. A. C., Abraham, C., and Kok, G. (2001). Scary warnings and rational precautions: A review of the psychology of fear appeals. *Psychology and Health,* 16, 613-630.

Ruiter, R. A. C., Kessels, L. T. E., Jansma, B. M., and Brug, J. (2006). Increased attention for computer-tailored health communications: An event-related potential study. *Health Psychology,* 25, 300-306.

Ruiter, R. A. C., and Kok, G. (2005). Saying is not (always) doing: Cigarette warning labels are useless. *European Journal of Public Health*, 15, 329-330.

Ruiter, R. A. C., and Kok, G. (2006). Response to Hammond et al. Showing leads to doing, but doing what? The need for experimental pre-testing. *European Journal of Public Health*, 16, 225.

Sanders, A. F. (1997). A summary of resources theories from a behavioral perspective. *Biological Psychology*, 45, 5-18.

Sherman, D. A. K., Nelson, L. D., and Steele, C. M. (2000). Do messages about health risks threaten the self? Increasing the acceptance of threatening health messages via self-affirmation. *Personality and Social Psychology Bulletin*, 26, 1046-1058.

Skinner, C. S., Campbell, M. K., Rimer, B. K., Curry, S., and Prochaska, J. O. (1999). How effective is tailored print communication? *Annals of Behavioral Medicine*, 21, 290-298.

Smith, N. K., Cacioppo, J. T., Larsen, J. T., and Chartrand, T. L. (2003). May I have your attention, please: Electrocortical responses to positive and negative stimuli. *Neuropsychologia*, 41, 171-183.

Srinivasan, R. (2004). High-Resolution EEG: Theory and Practice. In T. C. Handy (Ed.), *Event-Related potentials: A methods handbook* (pp. 167-188). Cambridge, MA: The MIT press.

Taubman - Ben-Ari, O., Florian, V., and Mikulincer, M. (2000). Does a threat appeal moderate reckless driving? A terror management theory perspective. *Accident Analysis and Prevention*, 32, 1-10.

Taylor, S. E. (1991). Asymmetrical effects of positive and negative events: The mobilization-minimization hypothesis. *Psychological Bulletin*, 110, 67-85.

Terry-McElrath, Y., Wakefield, M., Ruel, E., Balch, G. I., Emery, S., Szczypka, G., Clegg-Smith, K., Flay, B. (2005). The Effect of Antismoking Advertisement Executional Characteristics on Youth Comprehension, Appraisal, Recall, and Engagement. *Journal of Health Communication*, 10, 127-143.

Thomsen, S. R., and Fulton, K. (2007). Adolescents' attention to responsibility messages in magazine alcohol advertisements: An eye-tracking approach. *The Journal of Adolescent Health* 41, 27-34.

Thrasher, J. F., Rousu, M. C., Hammond, D., Navarro, A., and Corrigan, J. R. (2011). Estimating the impact of pictorial health warnings and "plain" cigarette packaging: Evidence from experimental auctions among adult smokers in the United States. *Health Policy*, 102, 41-48.

Thrasher, J. F., Rousu, M. C., Anaya-Ocampo, R., Reynales-Shigematsu, L. M., Arillo-Santillán, E., and Hernández-Ávila, M. (2007). Estimating the impact of different cigarette package warning label policies: The auction method. *Addictive Behaviors*, 32, 2916-2925.

Thrasher, J., Villalobos, V., Szklo, A., Fong, G., Pérez, C., and Sebrié, E. (2010). Assessing the impact of cigarette package warning labels: a cross-country comparison in Brazil, Uruguay and Mexico. *Salud Pública de México*, 52, S206-215.

Van Koningsbruggen, G. M., and Das, E. (2009). Don't derogate this message! Self-affirmation promotes online type 2 diabetes risk test taking. *Psychology and Health*, 24, 635-649.

Van Koningsbruggen, G. M., Das, E., and Roskos-Ewoldsen, D. R. (2009). How self-affirmation reduces defensive processing of threatening health information: Evidence at the implicit level. *Health Psychology*, 28, 563-568.

Whitehead, D., and Russell, G. (2004). How effective are health education programmes--resistance, reactance, rationality and risk? Recommendations for effective practice. *International Journal of Nursing Studies*, 41, 163-172.

Wilson, T. D. (2002). *Strangers to ourselves: Discovering the adaptive unconscious*. Cambridge, MA: The Belknap Press of Harvard University Press.

Wilson, T. D., and Dunn, E. W. (2004). Self-knowledge: Its limits, value and potential for improvement. *Annual Review of Psychology*, 55, 493-518.

Witte, K. (1992). Putting the fear back into fear appeals: The extended parallel process model. *Communication Monographs*, 59, 329-349.

Witte, K., and Allen, M. (2000). A meta-analysis of fear appeals: Implications for effective public health campaigns. *Health Education and Behavior*, 27, 591-615.

Witte, K., Berkowitz, J. M., Cameron, K. A., and McKeon, J. K. (1998). Preventing the spread of genital warts: Using fear appeals to promote self-protective behaviors. *Health Education and Behavior*, 25, 571-585.

Woodgate, J., and Brawley, L. R. (2008). Use of an efficacy-enhancing message to influence the self-regulatory efficacy of cardiac rehabilitation participants: A field experiment. *Rehabilitation Psychology*, 53, 153-161.

In: Psychology of Threat   ISBN: 978-1-62257-344-8
Editors: B. Hunter and T. Romero   © 2013 Nova Science Publishers, Inc.

Chapter 3

DIVERSITY IS BLISS: HOW A MIXTURE OF PERSONALITY TRAITS IN GROUP CONTEXTS MAY PROMOTE OUR SURVIVAL

Tsachi Ein-Dor [*] *and Adi Perry*

Interdisciplinary Center Herzliya, School of Psychology, Herzliya, Israel

Abstract

When God looked upon man, He or She contended that, "It is not good for the man to be alone." (Genesis, 2:18). As humans, we lack the physical strength of true predators, or the speed of those hunted by them; our strength lies in our combined efforts to overcome threat. Research on group-level reactions to threat, however, is scarce. In this contribution, we will review theory and research on social defense theory (SDT) – a theory that tries to shed light on human reactions to threat from a group-level perspective. SDT suggests that dispositional variables such as attachment orientations may influence people's responses under conditions of threat and related-stress. Some individuals (those scoring relatively high on measures of attachment anxiety) are chronically hypervigilant and alert to potential threats and dangers; they have heightened mental accessibility to what my colleagues and I call sentinel-related schemas, which allow them to detect threats sooner than others and communicate these threats to other members of their group. Other individuals (those scoring relatively high on measures of attachment-related avoidance) are less vigilant to threat than their anxious counterparts; yet, once alerted to a threat, they are likely to take protective action

* *E-mail address: teindor@idc.ac.il; School of Psychology, Interdisciplinary Center, P.O.Box 167, Herzliya, 46150, Israel. (Corresponding author)

more rapidly and effectively than others. Finally, people scoring relatively low on measures of attachment anxiety and avoidance (i.e., the relatively secure ones) are likely to lead and manage collective efforts to deal with threats, although they are less vigilant to threats than anxious individuals and slower to respond to threats than avoidant individuals. Because each of these personality patterns contributes to effective responses, SDT predicts that groups containing all three kinds of people will be more effective than less heterogeneous groups when dealing with threats and dangers. That is, heterogeneous groups may exhibit early threat detection, rapid response generation, and effective cooperation.

When God looked upon man, He or She contended that, "It is not good for the man to be alone."(Genesis, 2:18). Indeed, our human physiology, which was perfected by evolution, does not allow us to effectively engage in fight-or-flight reactions to threat. We do not share the sheer strength of other animals to face danger by ourselves, nor the speed to escape it. Our strength stems from our social entity. Theory and research have indeed indicated that in the course of evolution, humans lived in small, highly interactive groups of kin, and formed complex social relationships, which are unique among mammals. Because social solutions to adaptive challenges were so crucial for human survival, many of our psychological mechanisms undoubtedly evolved to support this aspect of human existence (Buss, 1995).

Brewer and Caporael (1990), as well as other scholars (e.g., Alexander, 1987; Axelrod, 1984; Cosmides, 1989; Gazzaniga, 2008), have argued that living in cooperative groups was the primary survival strategy for humans. Nevertheless, most of the research on human reactions to threats focuses on the individual level of analysis and examines mental processes such as threat perception and coping (e.g., Brandtstadter, Voss, and Rothermund, 2004) or immediate self-preservation responses such as fight or flight (e.g., Brown, 1954). There is good reason to believe, however, that psychological reactions to threats are not isolated from the social context, including the groups in which people find themselves. In the present contribution, we would attempt to probe the complexity of human reaction to threat by presenting social defense theory (SDT; Ein-Dor, Mikulincer, Doron, and Shaver, 2010), which is based on the possibility that individuals will respond to threat based partly on dispositional variables. Some individuals are chronically hypervigilant and constantly alert to potential threats and dangers. Other individuals, once alerted to a threat, are self-reliant and likely to take protective action rapidly and effectively. Still other individuals are relationship oriented and likely to be leaders, coordinators, and managers of collective efforts. Because each one of these personality patterns contributes to effective reactions in times of danger, SDT predicts that groups containing all three kinds of people will be more effective when dealing with threats and dangers (early detection, rapid response, and effective cooperation) than less heterogeneous groups. In the initial outline of SDT (Ein-Dor et al., 2010), these personality patterns were people's attachment orientations.

Bowlby's attachment theory (1973, 1980, 1982) proposes that human beings possess an innate psychobiological system (*the attachment behavioral system*) that motivates them to seek the aid of others – a socially based solution – when they need protection from threats and dangers. When people experience their caregivers as responsive and supportive, they develop a sense of attachment security, along with constructive strategies (e.g., support-seeking) for coping with threats and regulating emotions. Conversely, when caregivers are perceived as unavailable or unreliable, a person tends to develop an insecure attachment orientation marked by either attachment-system hyperactivating strategies (attachment anxiety) or attachment-system deactivating strategies for regulating emotions and social behavior (avoidant attachment). The different attachment orientations are measurable in infancy, childhood, and adulthood, and their causes and psychological consequences have been extensively studied (see Cassidy and Shaver, 2008; and Mikulincer and Shaver, 2007, for recent reviews).

Social and personality psychologists generally conceptualize adult attachment patterns as regions in a continuous two-dimensional space (e.g., Brennan, Clark, and Shaver, 1998). One dimension, attachment-related *anxiety*, reflects the extent to which a person worries that others will not be available or helpful in times of need. People high on attachment anxiety exaggerate their sense of vulnerability and insistently call on others for help and care, sometimes to the point of being intrusive (e.g., Feeney and Noller, 1990). The second dimension, attachment-related *avoidance*, reflects the extent to which a person distrusts relationship partners' goodwill, strives to maintain independence, and relies on deactivating strategies for dealing with threats and negative emotions. Avoidant people cope with threats by deemphasizing distress and vulnerability and by attempting to cope independently, without seeking others' help (e.g., Fraley and Shaver, 1997).

Attachment security is defined by low scores on both anxiety and avoidance. Secure people generally cope with threats by relying on internal resources developed with the help of security-enhancing attachment figures or by effectively seeking support from others or collaborating with them (Shaver and Mikulincer, 2002).

Secure individuals generally have high self-esteem, trust other people, and perceive the world as a relatively safe place (see Mikulincer and Shaver, 2007, for a review). According to both theory and research, attachment security confers adaptive advantages, compared with insecurity, in a variety of social, emotional, and behavioral domains (Mikulincer and Shaver, 2007). For example, secure individuals tend to have more lasting and satisfying close relationships as well as fewer psychological problems. They are also viewed by others as more ideal relationship partners (e.g., Klohnen and Luo, 2003).

These benefits of security caused researchers to wonder why a substantial portion of all large samples studied in various countries are insecure with respect to attachment. Belsky and colleagues were the first to argue that under certain conditions attachment insecurity has adaptive benefits, because it is associated with earlier menarche in females and earlier reproduction (e.g., Belsky, Steinberg, Houts, and Halpern-Felsher, 2010).

Theory and research also suggest, however, that survival rather than early reproduction might be the major reason for the emergence of the attachment behavioral system during mammalian, especially primate, evolution (Cassidy and Shaver, 2008; Ein-Dor et al., 2010). Threats (e.g., natural signs of danger or threats to a close relationship; Bowlby, 1982) activate the attachment system, which is adaptive because it increases the likelihood of protection, support, and survival (e.g., Mikulincer, Birnbaum, Woddis, and Nachmias, 2000; Mikulincer, Gillath, and Shaver, 2002). Therefore, Ein-Dor and colleagues (2010) proposed social defense theory, which is based on the possibility that each of the major attachment orientations (secure, anxious, and avoidant) confers unique adaptive advantages that increase the *inclusive fitness* (see Hamilton, 1964) of members of groups that include insecure as well as secure attachment patterns.

These advantages might also contribute to group-level selection (e.g., Wilson, Vugt, and O'Gorman, 2008), although group-level selection remains controversial (see Ein-Dor et al., 2010).

Social Defense Theory

According to SDT (Ein-Dor et al., 2010), each of the three major attachment patterns– secure, anxious, and avoidant – confers special adaptive advantages that tend to increase the inclusive fitness of people in groups that contain members of all three kinds. Each pattern also has distinct disadvantages, which may decrease inclusive fitness if they are not complemented by contributions by people with different attachment styles. This view is in line with Nettle's argument on general personality variations that can be understood in terms of tradeoffs among fitness costs and benefits: "Behavioral alternatives can be considered as tradeoffs, with a particular trait producing not unalloyed advantage but a mixture of costs and benefits such that the optimal value for fitness may depend on very specific local circumstances" (Nettle, 2006, p. 625).

Advantages and Disadvantages of Secure Individuals

Attachment research has shown that secure individuals benefit the groups to which they belong. For example, they are generally better than insecure people at leading and coordinating group activities (Davidovitz, Mikulincer, Shaver, Ijzak, and Popper, 2007) and work more effectively with other group members when solving problems (Rom and Mikulincer, 2003; Smith, Murphy, and Coats, 1999). According to Mikulincer and Shaver's (2003, 2007) literature reviews, these advantages stem from a sense of security rooted in past supportive experiences with attachment figures. This sense of security is closely associated with core beliefs, such as the belief that the world is a safe place, especially when significant others are present. These optimistic, comforting mental representations promote self-soothing reappraisals of threats, which help secure individuals perform better than insecure ones in many challenging situations (see Cassidy and Shaver, 2008, and Mikulincer and Shaver, 2007 for extensive reviews).

What attachment researchers call "felt security" (Sroufe and Waters, 1977), however, does not always reflect actual physical security. In times of danger, a sense of felt security can be maladaptive if it hinders rapid recognition of a threat or retards assembly of a rapid, effective response. For example, Mawson (1978, 1980, 2005) showed that the typical human response to danger is to seek the proximity of familiar people and places, even if this means remaining in or even approaching a dangerous situation (see also Baker and Chapman, 1962; Henderson, 1977; Kinston and Rosser, 1974). Secure individuals may activate schemas and scripts that promote seeking proximity to others (e.g., Mikulincer et al., 2002; Mikulincer, Shaver, Sapir-Lavid, and Avihou-Kanza, 2009; Waters and Waters, 2006), even though this is sometimes not the safest strategy. Such proximity-seeking in cases of actual danger may have two disadvantages: (a) slower identification of early signs of danger and (b) slower activation of defensive behavior.

Sime (1983, 1985) examined these disadvantages in a retrospective study of reactions to a fire in a large coastal resort on the Isle of Man, Great Britain, in 1973. He found that people who were physically closer to significant others (e.g., family members) were less likely to react to ambiguous cues of danger, such as noises and shouts, which occurred during the early stages of the fire. They reacted only later, when unambiguous cues of danger, such as smoke, flames, and people running while holding fire extinguishers, occurred. Subsequent studies of survivors' behavior during disasters also suggest that people who were together with familiar others were slow to perceive that they were in danger (Aguirre, Wenger, and Vigo, 1998; Fitzpatrick and Mileti, 1991; Perry, 1994; Proulx, 2002, 2003). For example, a study on the September 11 attacks (Fahy and Proulx, 2005), has revealed that most of the World-Trade-Center-2 (WTC-2) occupants commonly reported first becoming aware of the event from visual cues (66%) such as fire, debris and smoke. Other reported first becoming aware of the event from more ambiguous cues as sounds and smells, which are commonly present before the unambiguous visual cues of danger. According to SDT, the tendency to classify ambiguous cues of danger as nonthreatening might be manifested by secure people's sense of security and safety.

Research examining reactions to real or imagined dangers also provides indirect support for the hypothesis that securely attached people react in nonoptimal way to signs of danger – i.e., react slowly to danger following its detection as compared with less secure individuals. For example, Bowlby (1973, p. 91) noted that during and after disasters, "no member of a family is content, or indeed able to do anything else, until all members of the family are gathered together." Studies of behavior during fires also show that people tend to converge and cluster (Bryan, 1985, 2002; Sime, 1983, 1985). Governments and trained professionals have great difficulty getting people to evacuate before and during disasters, because "traditional family ties often keep individual members in the danger zone until it is too late" (Hill and Hansen, 1962, p. 217). For example, a study on the 9/11 attacks has indicated that about half of the WTCs occupants stated that they started their evacuation immediately after they sensed that something has gone wrong. Others, however, mentioned some delay to get organized or to receive instructions. One group stayed in a room discussing the situation for approximately 1 hour before deciding to evacuate the building. According to SDT, the tendency to work in teams, to get organized, and to wait for instructions and guidelines, which may be effective but demands time, may be more pronounced among more secure people than in their less secure counterparts.

Taken together, the evidence suggests that although secure people with respect to attachment are better at leading and coordinating group activities, these advantages are partially offset by their slower identification of actual and imminent dangers and their sometimes nonoptimal reactions to danger because of their wish to stay close to other people. This suggests that the tendency of secure people to focus on an ongoing project irrespective of mounting danger may sometimes hamper their survival and the survival of their group. Vigilance to danger and a quick fight-or-flight response are sometimes necessary to avert disaster. People high on either attachment anxiety or attachment avoidance might confer these abilities.

Advantages and Disadvantages of People High on Attachment Avoidance

Avoidant people adopt distancing ways of coping with stress, and deemphasize distress and vulnerability (e.g., Fraley and Shaver, 1997).Therefore, they might be less vigilant to threat and perceive that they are in danger later than others. They do not perform well as teammates, and have lower expectations of contributing to the team effort (Rom and Mikulincer, 2003). In times of need, they are accustomed to looking out for their own interests and taking care of themselves, even if this sometimes occurs at other people's expense (e.g., B. Feeney and Collins, 2001); thus, they are more likely to rely on self-protective fight-or-flight responses in times of danger, without hesitating or needing to deliberate with other group members, a reaction that Ein-Dor and colleagues (2010) coined *rapid fight-or-flight behavior*. This defensive pattern has both disadvantages and advantages. In the face of danger, avoidant individuals may be primarily motivated to save themselves, but this tendency may allow them to quickly discover a way to do so. Meanwhile, anxiously and securely attached individuals may focus much of their attention on the whereabouts and welfare of close associates without focusing quickly and fully on how to escape.

Imagine an avoidant person in the presence of a dangerous fire. While taking quick protective action, the person may find an escape route or take effective action to put out the fire or seal a door to keep the fire outside. Moreover, the avoidant people may be personally effective because they are not overwhelmed by emotion when drastic action is required. Although there are obvious moral dangers in behaving this way, there is little doubt that it can increase an avoidant person's survival chances while sometimes saving other people's lives, including the lives of group members about whom the avoidant individual may not care very deeply. Evidence for the influence of a few group members' early decisions to flee a dangerous situation can be found in the research literatures on military situations and natural disasters. One of the most alarming sights for human beings is other people running from danger (e.g., Mawson, 1980). As Marshall (1947) eloquently stated in writing about military behavior during World War II: "It can be laid down as a general rule that nothing is more likely to collapse a line of infantry than the sight of a few of its number in full and unexplained flight to the rear... One or two or more men made a sudden run to the rear which others in the vicinity did not understand... In every case the testimony of all witnesses clearly [indicated] that those who started the run... had a legitimate or at least a reasonable excuse for the action" (pp. 145-146). It is also known that in dangerous situations people tend to follow the route they see others taking (Mawson, 1980). Individuals who flee first (those, according to SDT, who are likely to be disproportionately avoidant) often clear a way by opening emergency doors, breaking a window, or finding a safer place to hide. When their escape route is identified and cleared, others can follow and take advantage of the escape route. Thus, avoidant individuals may increase their own and their group members' chances of survival under emergency conditions.

According to SDT, this behavior is stemming from a particular kind of schema regarding ways to cope with threats – a rapid fight-or-flight schema. According to Rumelhart (1980), self-schemas consist of a number of "placeholders" that supply default behaviors for certain kinds of situations. Possessing this kind of schema helps a person respond quickly to relevant situations, and if the situation provides insufficiently detailed information about how to respond, the default strategy can be quickly adopted. SDT contends that the schemas of people high on attachment avoidance contain something like the following placeholders: (a) minimize the importance of threatening stimuli; (b) when danger is clearly imminent, take quick self-protective action, either by escaping the situation or by taking action against the danger; and (c) at such times, do not worry about coordinating one's efforts with those of other people. In support of this notion, Ein-Dor and colleagues (2011a) found that attachment avoidance was associated with high access to core components of the rapid fight-or-flight schema when writing a story about threatening events. This schema comprised five components: (a) escaping a situation without helping others, (b) acting without receiving help from others, (c) reacting quickly without depending on other people's actions, (d) lack of cooperation with others, and (e) lack of deliberation with others. More avoidant participants recognized more recently encountered rapid fight-or-flight-schema information, reacted quicker than people low on attachment avoidance to rapid fight-or-flight-related information, and were prone to 'recall' schema-biased false memories. After reading a rapid fight-or-flight oriented vignette, participants who scored higher on attachment avoidance were more likely to generate more inferences and conjectures than people low on attachment avoidance. Across all studies, attachment avoidance scores were not associated with processing threat-*irrelevant* information. Moreover, the effects of attachment avoidance were not explained by individual differences in attachment-unrelated verbal and memory abilities, speed of recognizing attachment-irrelevant information, or attachment-unrelated inference skills. Also, the findings were not explained by general personality traits (e.g., neuroticism, extraversion) or by scores on a measure of socially desirable responding. Instead, they were unique to individual differences in the attachment domain.

Ein-Dor and Perry (in preparation) extended this work and examined whether people high on attachment avoidance adopt action tendencies associated with the rapid fight-or-flight schema. Specifically, participants were asked to complete the Blanchard and colleagues' (2001) threat scenario questionnaire, which comprise twelve threat-related scenarios (e.g., "It is past midnight and you are walking through an unfamiliar part of town. As you round a corner, you accidentally run into a man. He becomes angry and shoves you."; "You are sleeping in bed during the night, but suddenly wake up thinking you have heard a suspicious noise. It is dark and you are alone."). Participants were asked to choose a response to each of these scenarios from the relatively comprehensive list of 10 response options. In line with predictions, they found that attachment avoidance was related with higher prevalence of fight responses in response to threat, as attack or struggle, and with a lower prevalence of non-fight-or-flight responses, as yelling, screaming and calling for help. Ein-Dor and colleagues (2011b) also examined whether attachment avoidance is associated with rapid fight-or-flight-related behaviors. Specifically, they examined whether in threatening situations, people who score high on attachment avoidance would respond quickly to a threat that has been detected (a room gradually filling up with smoke, apparently because of a malfunctioning computer); and this quick reaction might increase the survival chances of all group members. In line with predictions, they found that attachment-related avoidance was associated with speedier escape responses to the danger once it was detected and therefore with greater group effectiveness. The results remained significant even when extraversion and neuroticism were statistically controlled. Thus, research has supported SDT's premise that attachment avoidance is associated with rapid fight-or-flight-related cognitions and behaviors.

More recently, Ein-Dor and colleagues (under review) examined whether the self-oriented way of copying that people high on attachment avoidant share, influence their metabolic processes. Socially oriented people can manage their energy more efficiently (Beckes and Coan, 2011) because they can share with other people the care for young (e.g., Ehrenberg, Gearing-Small, Hunter, and Small, 2001), assist in times of need (e.g., Townsend and Franks, 1995), share resources (e.g., Roger and De Boar, 2001), and contribute vigilance for potential threat (Davis, 2010; Ein-Dor et al., 2011a). Because avoidant people do not share the cost of many of life's metabolically expensive activities with others (Beckes and Coan, 2011), they might need to maintain greater metabolic resources to make decisions, engage in problem solving, and regulate their vigilance for potential threat. In other words, people high on attachment avoidance might maintain greater fasting basal glucose level, our metabolic fuel (Vannucci and Vannucci, 2000).

Ein-Dor and colleagues (under review) found that women who chronically tend to distance themselves from social ties – those high on attachment avoidance – maintained greater fasting basal glucose than more socially oriented women. In a second study they replicated this result in a different culture (Israel as compared to United States of America), among women as well as men from a different age group (adults and late adults as compared to young adults), and with a different measure to tap attachment avoidance. Thus, the association between social avoidance and basal glucose level seems robust. These findings were not explained by elevated tension and stress that might be experienced by avoidant people. Greater levels of basal glucose may be manifested by tension and stress because an elevated level of basal glucose is one of the markers of stress in many species of animals as well as in humans (e.g., Armario, Marti, Molina, Pablo, and Valdes, 1996). Research has indicated that a small and unsupportive social network, as well as the sense of loneliness, may trigger overwhelming amounts of tension and stress (e.g., Bowlby, 1973). The findings indicated, however, that the association between attachment avoidance and basal glucose level remained significant even after controlling for three sensitive indicators of tension and distress: self-report level of anxiety, hypertension disorder, and cortisol/adrenal androgen dehydroepiandrosterone (DHEA) ration (which has been repeatedly associated with tension, stress, and other related psychopathology; see Goodyer, Park, Netherton, and Herbert, 2001 for a review).

Advantages and Disadvantages of People High on Attachment Anxiety

As compared with people who are secure with respect to attachment, those who score higher on anxious attachment often perform relatively poorly in groups (Rom and Mikulincer, 2003). They may take the work less seriously, make fewer or poorer-quality contributions to a team, and have lower expectations of contributing to the team effort. Nevertheless, the strategies characteristically used by anxious people to deal with threats may be beneficial to inclusive fitness in certain kinds of threatening situations. Anxious people are vigilant in monitoring the environment for threats and are emotionally expressive and desirous of support when a threat is detected (e.g., Cassidy and Kobak, 1988; Feeney and Noller, 1990). They may benefit other people in their social surroundings by reacting quickly and vocally to early, perhaps ambiguous, cues of danger, a reaction that Ein-Dor and colleagues (2010) coined *sentinel behavior*. According to SDT, this behavior is stemming from a particular kind of schema regarding ways to cope with threats – a sentinel schema. SDT contends that the schemas of people high on attachment anxiety contain default placeholders that cause them (a) to remain vigilant with respect to possible threats, especially in unfamiliar or ambiguous situations; (b) to react quickly and strongly to early, perhaps unclear cues of danger (e.g., unusual noises, shuffling feet, shouts); (c) to alert others about the imminent danger; (d) if others are not immediately supportive, to heighten efforts to get them to provide support; and (e) to minimize distance from others when coping with a threat (Ein-Dor, Mikulincer, and Shaver, 2011a). Many species of animals benefit from having sentinels in their midst. For instance, various mammals (e.g., Fichtel, 2004), and primates (e.g., Coss, Ramakrishnan, and Schank, 2005; Riede, Bronson, Hatzikirou, and Zuberbuhler, 2005) produce shrill alarm signals when they detect a potential threat. In similar ways, human group members can benefit from anxious individuals' hyperactivating strategies.

In support of this notion, Ein-Dor and colleagues (2011a) found that attachment anxiety was associated with high access to core components of the sentinel schema (noticing danger before other people do, warning others about the danger) when writing a story about threatening events. More anxious participants remembered (i.e., recognized) more recently encountered sentinel-schema information, reacted quicker than their more secure counterparts to sentinel-related information, and were prone to 'recall' schema-biased false memories. After reading a sentinel oriented vignette, participants who scored higher on attachment anxiety were more likely to generate more inferences and conjectures than people low on attachment anxiety. Finally, it was found that the most attachment-anxious person in a group was more likely than other group members to quickly detect a threat (smoke from a malfunctioning computer). These effects were not explained by individual differences in attachment-unrelated verbal and memory abilities, speed of recognizing attachment-irrelevant information, or attachment-unrelated inference skills. Also, the findings were not explained by general personality traits (e.g., neuroticism, extraversion) or by scores on a measure of socially desirable responding. Instead, they were unique to individual differences in the attachment domain.

Ein-Dor and Perry (in preparation) extended this work and examined whether people high on attachment anxiety adopt action tendencies associated with the sentinel schema. In line with predictions, they found that attachment anxiety was related with lower prevalence of fight-or-flight responses in response to threat, as attack or struggle, but with a higher prevalence of sentinel responses, as yelling, screaming and calling for help.

In another research project, Ein-Dor, Mikulincer and Shaver (2011b) examined whether attachment anxiety is associated with sentinel-related behaviors. Specifically, they examined whether in threatening situations, people who score high on attachment anxiety may react emotionally and thereby alert other group members to the danger and the need for protection or escape. To test these predictions, 46 groups of 3 people were unobtrusively observed in a threatening laboratory situation: a room gradually filling up with smoke, apparently because of a malfunctioning computer. In line with predictions, they found that attachment anxiety was associated with quicker detection of the smoke in the room and therefore with greater group effectiveness. The results remained significant even when extraversion and neuroticism, two possible confounds, were statistically controlled.

More recently, Ein-Dor and Orgad (under review) extended these results and examined whether people high on attachment anxiety also share a heightened tendency to deliver a warning message without delay following a detection of threat. They led participants to believe that they accidently activated a computer virus that erased the experimenter's computer. Then, participants were asked to alert the departments' computer technicians to the incident. On their way, participants were presented with four decision points where they could choose either to delay their warning or to continue directly to the technicians' office. Results indicated that people high in attachment anxiety were less willing to be delayed on their way to deliver a warning message than their more secure counterparts. This result remained significant when attachment avoidance, extroversion and neuroticism were statistically controlled. Thus, research has supported SDT's premise that attachment anxiety is associated with sentinel-related cognitions and behaviors.

Group Composition and Its Association with Effectiveness When Dealing with Threat

SDT contend that secure and insecure attachment styles may have both unique adaptive advantages (which increase inclusive fitness) and disadvantages (which decrease inclusive fitness), and hence may have different benefits for group members under threatening conditions. This suggests that a group that contains people with different attachment patterns – secure, anxious, and avoidant members – might be superior to other groups in dealing with threats and survival problems. Groups marked by attachment-style diversity should detect potential problems and threats quickly (with anxious members acting as sentinels); act quickly without much deliberation, negotiation, or compromise (with avoidant members serving as models of rapid self-protection); and manage complex social tasks (with secure members acting as leaders and coordinators of the group).

To date, this proposition was directly tested in a single study by Ein-Dor and colleagues (2011b). They observed 46 groups of 3 people in a threatening laboratory situation: a room gradually filling up with smoke, apparently because of a malfunctioning computer. In line with predictions, they found that the more diverse a group in terms of attachment patterns, the more effective was the group. Pending on the ability to replicate this finding, the study highlights the potentially adaptive aspects of groups' composition with respect to attachment orientations.

Conclusion

SDT was devised to account for the social nature of human reactions to threats. It is based on the premise that people with different attachment patterns – secure, anxious, and avoidant members – bring different abilities into a group in which they find themselves in, and thus making it superior to other groups in dealing with threats and survival problems. Research has indicated that people high on attachment anxiety may act as sentinels that detect potential problems and threats quickly and alert others to those threats (Ein-Dor and Orgad, under review; Ein-Dor et al., 2011a, 2011b; Ein-Dor and Perry, in preparation).

People high on attachment avoidance may act quickly without much hesitation, which contribute to group effectiveness and promote their own survival as that of other people around them (Ein-Dor et al., 2011a, 2011b). Research has also indicated that avoidant people might have elevated metabolic fuel to support such individualistic behavior (Ein-Dor et al., under review).

Finally, more secure individuals (those low on both attachment anxiety and avoidance) manage complex social tasks better than their more insecure counterparts (Rom and Mikulincer, 2003), and cooperate better with other teammates. If SDT continues to receive empirical support, it my bear important implications for theory and research concerning group processes, threat detection, and our understanding of the adaptive aspects of personality variations.

References

Aguirre, B. E., Wenger, D., and Vigo, G. (1998). A test of the emergent norm theory of collective behavior. *Sociological Forum*, 13, 301–311.

Alexander, R. D. (1987). *The biology of moral systems*. New York: Aldine de Gruyter.

Armario, A., Marti, O., Molina, T., de Pablo, J., and Valdes, M. (1996). Acute stress markers in humans: response of plasma glucose, cortisol and prolactin to two examinations differing in the anxiety they provoke. *Psychoneuroendocrinology*, 21, 17-24.

Axelrod, R. (1984). *The evolution of cooperation*. New York: Basic Books.

Baker, G. W., and Chapman, D. W. (1962). *Man and society in disaster*. New York: Basic Books.

Beckes, L., and Coan, J. A. (2011). Social baseline theory: The role of social proximity in emotion and economy of action. *Social and Personality Psychology Compass*, 5, 976-988.

Belsky, J., Steinberg, L., Houts, R. M., and Halpern-Felsher, B. L. (2010). The development of reproductive strategy in females: Early maternal harshness → earlier menarche → increased sexual risk taking. *Developmental Psychology*, 46, 120-128.

Bowlby, J. (1973). *Attachment and loss: Vol. 2. Separation: Anxiety and anger*. New York: Basic Books.

Bowlby, J. (1980). *Attachment and loss: Vol. 3. Sadness and depression*. New York: Basic Books.

Bowlby, J. (1982). *Attachment and loss: Vol. 1. Attachment* (2nd ed.). New York: Basic Books. (Original ed. 1969).

Brandtstädter, J., Voss, A., and Rothermund, K. (2004). Perception of danger signals: The role of control. *Experimental Psychology*, 51, 24-32.

Brennan, K. A., Clark, C. L., and Shaver, P. R. (1998). Self-report measurement of adult romantic attachment: An integrative overview. In J. A. Simpson and W. S. Rholes (Eds.), *Attachment theory and close relationships* (pp. 46-76). New York: Guilford Press.

Brewer, M. B., and Caporael, L. R. (1990). Selfish genes vs. selfish people: Sociobiology as origin myth. *Motivation Emotion*, 14, 237–243.

Brown, R. W. (1954). Mass phenomena. In G. Lindzey (Ed.), *Handbook of social psychology* (pp. 833-876). Reading, Mass: Addison-Wesley.

Bryan, J. L. (1985). Convergence clusters: A phenomenon of human behavior seen in selected high-rise building fires. *Fire Journal,* 79(6), 27-30.

Bryan, J. L. (2002). A selected historical review of human behavior in fire. *Fire Protection Journal*, 16, 4–10.

Buss, D. M. (1995). Evolutionary psychology: A new paradigm for psychological science. *Psychological Inquiry*, 6, 1-30.

Cassidy, J., and Kobak, R. R. (1988). Avoidance and its relationship with other defensive processes. In J. Belsky and T. Nezworski (Eds.), *Clinical implications of attachment* (pp. 300-323). Hillsdale, NJ: Erlbaum.

Cassidy, J., and Shaver, P. R. (Eds.). (2008). *Handbook of attachment: Theory, research, and clinical applications* (2nd ed.). New York: Guilford Press.

Cosmides, L. (1989). The logic of social exchange: Has natural selection shaped how humans reason? Studies with the Wason selection task. *Cognition*, 31, 187-276.

Coss, R. G., Ramakrishnan, U., and Schank, J. (2005). Recognition of partially concealed leopards by wild bonnet macaques (Macacaradiata) the role of the spotted coat. *Behavioural Processes*, 68, 145-163.

Davidovitz, R., Mikulincer, M., Shaver, P. R., Ijzak, R., and Popper, M. (2007). Leaders as attachment figures: Their attachment orientations predict leadership-related mental representations and followers' performance and mental health. *Journal of Personality and Social Psychology*, 93, 632-650.

Davis, L. S. (2010). Alarm calling in Richardson's Ground Squirrels (Spermophilusrichardsonii). *Zeitschrift fur Tierpsychologie*, 66, 152–164.

Ehrenberg, M. F., Gearing-Small, M., Hunter, M. A., and Small, B. J. (2001). Childcare task division and shared parenting attitudes in dual-earner families with young children. *Family Relations*, 50, 143–153.

Ein-Dor, T., Mikulincer, M., Doron, G., and Shaver, P. R. (2010). The attachment paradox: How can so many of us (the insecure ones) have no adaptive advantages? *Perspectives on Psychological Science*, 5, 123-141.

Ein-Dor, T., Mikulincer, M., and Shaver, P. R. (2011a). Attachment insecurities and the processing of threat-related information: Studying the scripts involved in insecure people's coping strategies. *Journal of Personality and Social Psychology*, 101, 78-93.

Ein-Dor, T., Mikulincer, M., and Shaver, P. R. (2011b). Effective reaction to danger: Attachment insecurities predict behavioral reactions to an experimentally induced threat above and beyond general personality traits. *Social Psychological and Personality Science*, 2, 467-473.

Ein-Dor, T., and Orgad, T. (under review). Scared saviors: Evidence that people high on attachment anxiety are more effective in alerting others to threat. *Social Psychological and Personality Science*.

Ein-Dor, T., and Perry, A. (in preparation). Attachment insecurities and their action tendencies in response to threat.

Fahy, R. F., and Proulx, G. (2005). Analysis of published accounts of the World Trade Center evacuation. *National Institute of Standards and Technology* NCSTAR 1-7A.

Feeney, B. C., and Collins, N. L. (2001). Predictors of caregiving in adult intimate relationships: An attachment theoretical perspective. *Journal of Personality and Social Psychology*, 80, 972-994.

Feeney, J. A., and Noller, P. (1990). Attachment style as a predictor of adult romantic relationships. *Journal of Personality and Social Psychology*, 58, 281-291.

Fichtel, C. (2004). Reciprocal recognition in sifaka (Propithecusverreauxiverreauxi) and red fronted lemur (Eulemurfulvusrufus) alarm calls. *Animal Cognition*, 7, 45-52.

Fitzpatrick, C., and Mileti, D. S. (1991). Motivating public evacuation. *International Journal of Mass Emergencies and Disasters*, 9, 137–152.

Fraley, R. C., and Shaver, P. R. (1997). Adult attachment and the suppression of unwanted thoughts. *Journal of Personality and Social Psychology*, 73, 1080-1091.

Gazzaniga, M. S. (2008). *Human: The science behind what makes us unique*. New York: HarperCollins.

Goodyer, I. M., Park, R. J., Netherton, C. M., and Herbert J. (2001). Possible role of cortisol and dehydroepiandrosterone in human development and psychopathology. *British Journal of Psychiatry*, 179, 243-249.

Hamilton, W. D. (1964). The genetical evolution of social behaviour: I, II. *Journal of Theoretical Biology*, 7, 1-52.

Henderson, S. (1977). The social network, support and neurosis: The function of attachment in adult life. *British Journal of Psychiatry*, 131, 185-191.

Hill, R., and Hansen, D. A. (1962). Families in disasters. In G. W. Baker and D. W. Chapman (Eds.), *Man and society in disaster* (pp. 185-221). New York: Basic Books.

Kinston, W., and Rosser, R. (1974). Disasters: Effects on mental and physical health. *Journal of Psychosomatic Research*, 18, 437-456.

Klohnen, E. C., and Luo, S. (2003). Interpersonal attraction and personality: What is attractive-self similarity, ideal similarity, complementarily or attachment security? *Journal of Personality and Social Psychology*, 85, 709-722.

Marshall, S. L. A. (1947). *Men against fire*. NewYork: Morrow.

Mawson, A. R. (1978, August). *Panic behavior: A review and a new hypothesis.* Paper presented at the 9th World York: Doubleday, Doran and Company. Congress of Sociology. Uppsala, Sweden.

Mawson, A. R. (1980). Is the concept of panic for study purposes? In B. Levin (Ed.). *Behavior in fires.* National bureau of standards, special publication, proceedings of the second international seminar on behavior in fire emergencies.

Mawson, A. R. (2005). Understanding mass panic and other collective responses to threat and disaster. *Psychiatry: Interpersonal and Biological Processes,* 68(2), 95-113.

Mikulincer, M., Birnbaum, G., Woddis, D., and Nachmias, O. (2000). Stress and accessibility of proximity-related thoughts: Exploring the normative and intraindividual components of attachment theory. *Journal of Personality and Social Psychology,* 78, 509-523.

Mikulincer, M., Gillath, O., and Shaver, P. R. (2002). Activation of the attachment system in adulthood: Threat-related primes increase the accessibility of mental representations of attachment figures. *Journal of Personality and Social Psychology,* 83, 881-895.

Mikulincer, M., and Shaver, P. R. (2003). The attachment behavioral system in adulthood: Activation, psychodynamics, and interpersonal processes. In M. P. Zanna (Ed.), *Advances in experimental social psychology* (pp. 53-152). New York: Academic Press.

Mikulincer, M., and Shaver, P. R. (2007). *Attachment in adulthood: Structure, dynamics, and change.* New York: Guilford Press.

Mikulincer, M., Shaver, P. R., Sapir-Lavid, Y., and Avihou-Kanza, N. (2009). What's inside the minds of securely and insecurely attached people? The secure-base script and its associations with attachment-style dimensions. *Journal of Personality and Social Psychology,* 97, 615-633.

Nettle, D. (2006). The evolution of personality variation in humans and other animals. *American Psychologist,* 61, 622-631.

Perry, R. W. (1994). A model of evacuation compliance behavior. In R. R. Dynes and K. J. Tierney (Eds.), *Disasters, collective behavior, and social organization* (pp. 85–98). Newark, DE: University of Delaware Press.

Proulx, G. (2002, April 15–16). *Understanding human behavior in stressful situations.* Presented in workshop to identify innovative research needs to foster improved fire safety in the United States, National Academy of Sciences, Delegate Binder Section 7, Washington, DC.

Proulx, G. (2003). Researchers learn from World Trade Center survivors' accounts. *Construction Innovation,* 8(1), 1–3.

Riede, T., Bronson, E., Hatzikirou, B., and Zuberbühler, K. (2005). The production mechanisms of Diana monkey alarm calls: Morphological data and a model. *Journal of Human Evolution*, 48, 85–96.

Roger, S. J., and De Boer, D. D. (2001). Changes in wives' incomes effects on marital happiness, psychological wellbeing, and the risk of divorce. *Journal of Marriage and the Family*, 63, 458–472.

Rom, E., and Mikulincer, M. (2003). Attachment theory and group processes: The association between attachment style and group-related representations, goals, memories, and functioning. *Journal of Personality and Social Psychology*, 84, 1220-1235.

Rumelhart, D. E. (1980) Schemata: The building blocks of cognition. In R. J. Spiro et al. (Eds.), *Theoretical issues in reading comprehension* (pp. 33-58). Hillsdale, NJ: Lawrence Erlbaum.

Shaver, P. R., and Mikulincer, M. (2002). Attachment-related psychodynamics. *Attachment and Human Development,* 4, 133-161.

Sime, J. D. (1983). Affiliative behavior during escape to building exits. *Journal of Environmental Psychology*, 3, 21–41.

Sime, J. D. (1985). Movement toward the familiar: Person and place affiliation in a fire entrapment setting. *Environment and Behavior*, 17, 697–724.

Smith, E. R., Murphy, J., and Coats, S. (1999). Attachment to groups: Theory and management. *Journal of Personality and Social Psychology*, 77, 94–110.

Sroufe, L. A., and Waters, E. (1977). Attachment as an organizational construct. *Child Development,* 48, 1184-1199.

Townsend, A. L., and Franks, M. M. (1995). Binding ties: Closeness and conflict in adult children's caregiving relationships. *Psychology and Aging*, 10, 343–351.

Vannucci, R. C., and Vannucci, S., J. (2000). Glucose metabolism in the developing brain. *Seminars in Perinatology*, 24, 107-115.

Waters, H. S., and Waters, E. (2006). The attachment working models concept: Among other things, we build script-like representations of secure base experiences. *Attachment and Human Development*, 8, 185-198.

Wilson, D. S., Van Vugt, M., and O'Gorman, R. (2008). Multilevel selection theory and major evolutionary transitions. *Current Directions in Psychological Science*, 17, 6-9.

In: Psychology of Threat   ISBN: 978-1-62257-344-8
Editors: B. Hunter and T. Romero   © 2013 Nova Science Publishers, Inc.

Chapter 4

STEREOTYPE THREAT BEYOND THE LABORATORY: DO SINGLE-GENDER COLLEGES SIGNAL A SAFETY IN THE AIR?

Avi Ben-Zeev and *Nisaa Kirtman*

Department of Psychology, San Francisco State University, CA, US

Abstract

Laboratory findings have pointed to numerical under-representation as a "threat in the air" (Steele, 1997) that causes women to underperform in quantitative domains, even in the presence of a single man. This study was designed to examine whether a similar effect occurs outside the laboratory in ecologically rich environments. Women from a coed versus a single-gender college were assigned to threat and no-threat conditions at a third location. An ANCOVA with math-SAT as a covariate suggested that only the coed women were affected negatively by threat despite their single-gender counterparts' higher levels of math and gender identification; factors linked to heightened threat susceptibility. Following Yzerbyt, Muller, and Judd (2004), findings were qualified to include a math-SAT by stereotype threat interaction, which implied a more nuanced protective effect of single-gender schooling. Results are discussed in context of the cues hypothesis, Integrated Process model of stereotype threat, psychological essentialism, and policy ramifications.

* E-mail address: abenzeev@sfsu.edu; Tel: (415) 215-2848; Fax: (415) 338-2398; Address: Department of Psychology, San Francisco State University, 1600 Holloway Avenue, EP 301, San Francisco, California 94132-4168. (Corresponding author)

Keywords: Stereotype threat, cues hypothesis, coed college, single-gender
college

Stereotype Threat Beyond the Laboratory: Do Single-gender Colleges Signal a Safety in the Air?

Subtle situational cues, such as gender composition for women in math, science, and engineering (MSE), can be powerful triggers of *stereotype threat*, a type of social identity threat (e.g., Abrams & Hogg, 1999; Major & O'Brien, 2005; Tajfel & Turner, 1986), which occurs when members of devalued groups experience a fear of being evaluated through the lens of a negative stereotype (e.g., C. Steele, 1997; Murphy, C. Steele, & Gross, 2007). Recently, Murphy, C. Steele, and Gross (2007) provided compelling evidence that the salience of situational cues was complicit in women's underperformance in quantitative domains. Murphy et al.'s data supported a "cues hypothesis" – women from MSE backgrounds who viewed an MSE conference video in which women were outnumbered, showed heightened physiological vigilance (objective measures of identity) as well as a decreased sense of belongingness and overall lower desire to participate in the MSE conference (subjective measures of identity).

The numerical representation cue has been linked strongly to signaling intellectual threat in MSE women in several controlled empirical investigations. Inzlicht and Ben-Zeev (2000) have shown that women who identified highly with success and achievement in the math domain underperformed on a math, but not on a verbal, test when men were simply present in the testing environment. Furthermore, Inzlicht and Ben-Zeev found that women's underperformance was proportional to the number of men in the environment; which is in agreement with Murphy et al.'s more recent theorizing that the salience of situational cues might be complicit in women's underperformance in stigmatized domains. Evidence from Inzlicht and Ben-Zeev (2000) and from several laboratory studies that have since replicated and expanded upon the nature of the deleterious effect of being outnumbered on women's intellectual performance (Inzlicht & Ben-Zeev, 2003; Inzlicht &Good, 2006; Sekaquaptewa & Thompson, 2003) make it clear that gender composition is to be taken seriously as a cue for social identity threat in MSE women. The subtlety of gender composition as a trigger for stereotype threat is powerful – it is a "threat in the air" (C. Steele, 1997) – independent of women's interest, confidence, and proven achievement in MSE domains (Murphy et al., 2007).

These robust laboratory findings on the effects of gender composition on women's math performance beg the question of whether women in single-gender (vs. coed) educational institutions would show differential susceptibility to stereotype threat effects. This question is important given the implications of the aforementioned laboratory studies to ecologically rich educational environments and in conjunction with the cues hypothesis. In the present study, therefore, we investigated whether women at a single-gender college would show a differential pattern of performance under stereotype threat as compared to women from a sister coed college. It is reasonable to predict that women from a single-gender college would be more resilient to stereotype threat even if tested outside their institution and in mixed gender settings, because these women are part of an institutional culture in which women not only have the predominant numerical representation but also have access to larger number of female role models (see Dasgupta & Asgari, 2004) and tend to receive instructional feedback that communicates high standards for performance in stigmatized domains (e.g., Langdon, 2001; Astin & Sax, 1996; Tidball, Smith, Tidball, & Wolf-Wendel, 1999); factors that have been linked to increased resilience to stereotype threat (Cohen, C. Steele, & Ross, 1999; Huguet & Regner, 2007; Marx & Roman, 2002).

Of particular relevance is Dasgupta and Asgari's (2004) study, which showed that when women were in social contexts that afforded them with female leaders (in the lab as well as in women's colleges; single-gender versus coed), women were less likely to exhibit automatic stereotypic beliefs about their gender and that automatic gender stereotyping was mediated by the degree of exposure to female faculty. Furthermore, participating in male-dominated MSE classes generated an increase in automatic stereotypic beliefs among women at the coed college but not at the same-gender college; an effect mediated by instructor gender. As Dasgupta and Asgari (2004) argued, these data as a whole highlight the importance of institutional culture in affecting women's nonconscious gender-related beliefs. Additionally, there might be other potential protective factors that have yet to be explored in the context of comparing single-gender versus coed institutional cultures (e.g., Ambady, Paik, C. Steele, Owen-Smith, & Mitchell, 2004; Aronson, Fried, & Good, 2002; Rosenthal & Crisp, 2006; Good, Aronson, & Inzlicht, 2003;Johns, Schmader, & Martens, 2005; Martens, Johns, Greenberg, & Schimel, 2006).

Theprediction that women in single-gender colleges would be more resilient to threat effects is not obvious, however, for two main reasons. First, single-gender institutions tend to promote a heightened level of gender identification, as compared to coed educational environments (Lirgg, 1994; Shmurak, 1998; Trickett, Trickett, Castro, & Schaffner, 1982). Given that women with higher levels of gender identification have been shown to be more susceptible to stereotype threat effects (Schmader, 2002), it is possible that women from single-gender colleges, under conditions of stereotype threat, would be just as, or even more, affected by stereotype threat effects, especially if tested outside of their educational institution. Second, single-gender institutions tend to also promote a higher level of engagement in MSE careers (Sebrechts, 1992; Langdon, 2001) that might cause women to identify more with achievement in the math domain. Math identification is yet another factor that has been shown to moderate stereotype threat effects, such that high math identification has been associated with increased vulnerability to threat (Aronson, Lustina, Good, Keough, C. Steele, & Brown, 1999).

Examining stereotype threat effects beyond the laboratory and in single-gender versus coed educational institutions calls for a quasi-experimental design. This design is powerful ecologically but has obvious limitations. It would be impossible (and unwise) to randomly assign women to enroll in either a women's college or a coeducational one. However, as discussed previously there exist a number of studies that highlight institutional variables in single-gender colleges, such as a female majority, access to female role models, more frequent student-teacher interactions, and educational values that emphasize pursuing gender atypical careers, which affect student outcomes (Langdon, 2001; Astin & Sax, 1996; Tidball, Smith, Tidball, & Wolf-Wendel, 1999), while controlling for individual student characteristics. Given this body of work, it would be important to address self-selection in interpreting the data from the current investigation, but self-selection would not likely be the only factor that would explain performance differences as a function of threat across women from single-gender versus coed institutions.

In order to compare the relative resiliency of women from single-gender versus coed institutions to stereotype threat, we chose institutions that are as similar demographically and culturally as possible in relation to aforementioned factors. To this end, we selected female participants from two adjacent sister liberal arts colleges in Southern California: Scripps College (single-gender) and Pitzer College (coed) that have similar teacher to student ratios as well as posses an overall shared educational mission of providing liberal arts education according to the vision of the larger institution to which both colleges belong (The Claremont Colleges). We then assigned women to stereotype threat or no threat conditions (blind to their institutional affiliation) at a third location.

Determining causation would lie outside the scope of a quasi-experimental design, but data that point to a higher resiliency to stereotype threat among women from a single-gender college in mixed gender testing environments would: (a) serve to defy predictions based on current laboratory findings on the inextricable links between high gender and math identification to stereotype threat vulnerability as well as implications for identity bifurcation – or women's selective identification from feminine characteristics under threat (Pronin, C. Steele, & Ross, 2004); (b) contribute to and extend Murphy et al.'s (2007) cues hypothesis to an ecologically rich setting; (c) set the stage for further research that would explicate both institutional variables as well as potential individual differences (including self selection variables) that would be foundational for interventions aimed at supporting women who pursue MSE careers to perform to their full potential and that might well go beyond numerical representation; and finally (d) create a foundation for future investigations, which would focus on how to import and to adapt current educational practices as well as cultural norms from single-gender to mixed-gender educational settings and thus inform policy reform.

Method

Participants

A total of 88 undergraduate women volunteered to participate in exchange for course credit. The sample comprised of 45 and 43 women from Scripps (single-gender) and Pitzer (coed) College respectively. Male participants from Pitzer College were recruited as confederates to create mixed-gender settings in accordance with previous research (e.g., Inzlicht & Ben-Zeev, 2000) and to maintain ecological validity with regard to the predominately mixed-gender testing environments in the United States.

Design

We employed a 2 x 2 between-subjects factorial design. The factors were College Type (single-gender versus coed) and Stereotype Threat (threat vs. no threat).

Materials and Procedure

The testing took place in a classroom at the *Keck Joint Science Center*, a central science center (at the nexus of three colleges: Scripps, Pitzer, and Claremont-McKenna). Students from both colleges (single-gender and coed) were greeted by a female confederate (blind to their college of origin), randomly assigned to threat and no threat conditions, and then completed the Necessary Arithmetic Operations (NAO) test, which is a speeded math test, described below.

Male confederates from the coed college were used to create mixed-gender settings in all conditions. In the threat condition, NAO was introduced as a genuine test of logical and mathematical abilities. In the non-threat condition, the NAO was introduced as a bias-free aptitude test, by stating that women had performed just as well as men on this test in the past. Participants then completed the NAO, Gender Identification Measure, MIQ, and finally, a demographics form containing questions about participants' background and institutional affiliation before being debriefed.

The Necessary Arithmetic Operations (NAO) Test

This 30-item test requires people to indicate the order in which arithmetic operations (e.g., "addition then division") need to be used to solve multi-step arithmetical word problems (Ekstrom, French, & Harman, 1976). The NAO was used in this study because the speeded nature of this test makes it challenging. We intentionally did not use the quantitative GRE exam because we preferred an unfamiliar test that would not elicit as strong of a pre-conceived gender bias.

Gender Identification Measure

This questionnaire is a subscale of the Collective Self-Esteem Scale (Luhtanen & Crocker, 1992) that was modified by Schmader (2002) to assess gender identity, in the context of stereotype threat. It contains four items on a scale ranging from 1 (strongly disagree) to 5 (strongly agree), such as "Being a man/woman is an important part of my self-image." Participants' responses to the four items are averaged to form an index of gender identification.

Math Identification Measure

The MIQ is a questionnaire that assesses the importance of mathematics to individuals (Brown & Josephs, 1999). It contains five items ranging from disagree strongly (1) and agree strongly (7). Sample items are, "My math abilities are very important to me," and "I don't care at all if other people believe that I am good at math" (reverse scored).

Results

Gender and Math Identification

Consistent with the literature, women from the single-gender college showed higher levels of gender identification (M = 4.23, SE = .11) than did coed counterparts (M = 3.91, SE = .11), $F(1, 86)$ = 4.54, p< 0.05. This result could have been due to the kind of population that is drawn to women's colleges (self-selection), the single-gender college climate, or both. In either case, a higher level of gender identification using this same measure has been associated with a heightened susceptibility to stereotype threat effects in the past (Schmader, 2002). Women from the single-gender college also showed higher levels of MIQ scores (M = 5.84, SE = .22) than did the coed group (M = 5.04, SE = .22), $F(1, 86)$ = 6.72, p< .05. Higher math identification has been associated with heightened susceptibility to stereotype threat as well (Aronson et al., 1999).

The Effects of Stereotype Threat and College Type on Math Scores

Following C. Steele and Aronson's (1995) original examination of stereotype threat, we ran 2 (Stereotype Threat: threat/no threat) x 2 (College Type: single-gender/coed) analysis of covariance (ANCOVA) with number correct as the dependent variable and math-SAT score as the covariate.

The ANCOVA revealed significant main effects for College Type, $F(1, 83)$ = 10.09, p< .002 and Stereotype Threat, $F(1, 83)$ = 6.43, p< .01, as well as an interaction of Stereotype Threat and College Type, $F(1, 83)$ = 5.69, p< .02. Women from the single-gender college scored similarly in the threat condition (M = 26.54, SE = .79) and no-threat condition (M = 26.64, SE = .84). However, women from the coed college scored more poorly under threat (M = 21.86, SE = .85) than their female peers in the no-threat condition (M = 25.88, SE = .80). Simple effects analyses, showed that coed women under threat performed significantly worse compared to all other groups, all ps < .05. All other simple effects were non-significant.

We also ran a 2 (Stereotype Threat: threat/no-threat) x 2 (College Type: single-gender/coed) analysis of variance (ANOVA) with number correct as the dependent variable (that is, without using the math-SAT as a covariate). The results were almost identical except that the College Type x Stereotype Threat interaction effect showed a trend towards significance, $F(1, 84)$ = 3.08, p = .08. Simple effect analyses produced the same result: Only coed women under threat differed significantly from the other three groups, all ps <.05. The descriptives (without adjusting for math-SAT) are shown in Figure 1.

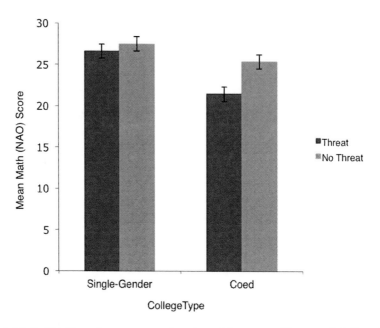

Figure 1. Math (NAO) performance as a function of Stereotype Threat and College Type.

Given the high level of performance on the NAO, there is a possibility that women in the single-gender college performed at ceiling, which in turn might have masked a potential threat effect when compared to the coed group. However, the fact that women from the same-gender college who were under no-threat performed similarly to the women from the coed college in both threat and no-threat conditions shows that the only individuals who were affected negatively by stereotype threat were the coed women under threat. Given that coed women under threat were the only ones who performed more poorly (as indicated by both the ANCOVA and ANOVA), it appears that the women from the two colleges were able to perform comparably on the math test. Nevertheless, it might be useful to employ an even more challenging math test in future investigations.

It is possible that the ANCOVA painted a partial picture that would be further illuminated by using regression. Specifically, we heeded Yzerbyt, Muller, and Judd's (2004) exhortation to examine whether the covariate (math-SAT) interacted with a grouping variable of interest (in this case, College Type). Yzerbyt et al. (2004) have made a compelling case that in stereotype threat studies researchers have neglected to take into account the fact that males tend to have higher mean math-SAT scores and greater variability. They reasoned thus that the math-SAT as a covariate would likely interact with gender (the relevant grouping variable) to create a biased estimate of the interaction between gender and stereotype threat.

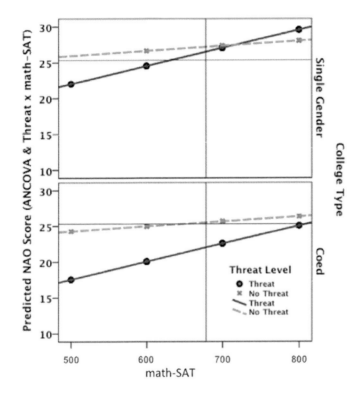

Figure 2. Predicted math (NAO) performance as a function of Stereotype Threat by math-SAT (separated by College Type).

In the current study we examined women only(men were used to create threat conditions and thus served as confederates) and given the exploratory and ecological nature of the current investigation we did not make *a priori* predictions about the need to account for math-SAT differences between women from the two sister colleges. However, we found that the mean math-SAT was different between women from the two colleges, favoring women from the single-gender college ($F(1, 86) = 9.82$, $p<.01$) (The majority of women in the single gender college scored in the 600-690 range, whereas the majority of women in the coed college scored in the 550-650 range). We therefore conducted additional analyses with Yzerbyt et al.'s (2004) caveat in mind.

Yzerbyt, Muller, and Judd's (2004) Procedure:
The Importance of Creating an Unbiased Estimate of an Interaction Effect and its Implications

We followed Yzerbyt et al.'s (2004) procedure for creating an unbiased estimate of an interaction effect with a covariate. To this end we ran two multiple regressions, as specified below. We contrast-coded the two levels of the grouping variable (College Type: single-gender as -1, coed as +1) and two levels of the experimentally manipulated variable (Stereotype Threat: threat as -1, no-threat as +1). The covariate math-SAT score was centered at the mean as was the criterion variable NAO score.

We first ran a multiple regression equivalent to the ANCOVA to obtain the coefficient and the p-value for the College Type x Stereotype Threat interaction term in a potentially mis-specified ANCOVA model. The standardized coefficients were significant for all the four terms entered – for College Type (β = -.301, t (82) = -3.176, p = .002), Stereotype Threat (β = .229, $t(82)$ = 2.536, p = .013), the College Type x Stereotype Threat interaction terms (β = .217, $t(82)$ = 2.386, p = .019) and the math-SAT score (β = .323, $t(82)$ = 3.344, p = .001).Next, we ran a regression analysis adding the College Type x math-SAT interaction term. The standardized coefficients remained significant for College Type (β = -.337, $t(82)$ = -3.532, p = .001), Stereotype Threat (β = .231, $t(82)$ = 2.601, p = .011), and math-SAT (β = .295, $t(82)$ = 3.065, p = .003), but became non-significant for the College Type x Stereotype Threat interaction term (β = .155, $t(82)$ = 1.628, p = .107) and marginally significant for the math-SAT x Stereotype Threat interaction term (β = -.176, $t(82)$ = -1.837, p = .070).

At face value, it appears that the College Type by Stereotype Threat interaction in the ANCOVA was due to the math-SAT by Stereotype Threat interaction. However, Yzerbyt et al.'s (2004) procedure actually provides a more nuanced interpretation of the data. Specifically, the negative coefficient for the math-SAT x Stereotype Threat interaction term in the corrected model, which was marginally significant, suggests that, for women with lower math-SAT scores (typically, women attending the coed college), the NAO score tended to be lower under threat than no-threat, whereas for women with higher math-SAT scores (typically, women attending the single-gender college), the NAO score tended to be higher under threat than no-threat. Please see Figure 2.

As can be seen in Figure 2, how a woman performs on the math-SAT is important to consider in terms of susceptibility/resilience to threat, but the findings cannot be summarized simply as: "Women with higher math-SAT skills are less susceptible to stereotype threat effects." Furthermore, if this were the case then the math-SATs for women from both colleges should be a robust predictor of their NAO score. However, upon conducting two separate regression analyses to examine whether women's SAT scores predicted their NAO score in each college, we found a significant effect for women from the same-gender college (β = .417, $t(43)$ = 3.006, p = .004) but only a marginally significant effect in women from the coed college (β = .287, $t(41)$ = 1.92, p = .062). Taken together, the data point to a more nuanced effect – a potential lift-like effect[1] under threat, mostly in women from the single-gender college (in addition to their math-SAT skill level) that may have resulted in part, from a challenge versus a threat appraisal to a math test as one possibility (e.g., Alter, Aronson, Darley, Rodriguez, & Ruble, 2010). This conjecture is based on the prevalence of MSE female role models (i.e., instructors) in single-gender versus coed colleges that have been shown to help negate negative automatic associations about women in MSE careers (see Dasgupta & Asgari, 2004) among other possible cultural aspects of these women's college experience. A high math-SAT score may be protective as serving as a correct pre-potent skill (see Jamieson & Harkins, 2007, *mere effort* account) but in and of itself does not seem sufficient for creating resilience to threat.

Discussion

The current study was a first step towards providing evidence that women from a single-gender college showed a "lift-like" effect to stereotype threat, beyond the protective effect of possessing pre-potent math-SAT skills, even when tested outside of their institution, and while maintaining high levels of math and gender identification. A single-gender institution appears to signal intellectual safety via cues that encompass more than numerical representation (Murphy et al., 2007) to include role models (Dasgupta & Asgari, 2004; Huguet & Regner, 2007; Marx &Roman, 2002) among other likely factors that have been linked to

---

[1]Walton and Cohen (2003) have shown that in a given stereotype threat study on women in math, male controls under threat did not tend to perform significantly better than male controls under no threat; but that across studies (using a meta analysis), men under threat demonstrated an upwards trend or a lift effect likely due to a downward comparison. However, whereas gender is usually visible; a woman's college affiliation in the sister colleges was not. In the context of the current study, all participants were tested at a third location and did not know which school the other students belonged to, if any (The Keck Science Center lies at the nexus of three colleges: Scripps, Pitzer, and Claremont McKenna). It is thus unlikely that the data were due to a lift effect *a la*Waltonand Cohen per se.

stereotype threat resiliency mostly in laboratory settings(e.g., Ambady, Paik, C. Steele, Owen-Smith, & Mitchell, 2004; Aronson, Fried, & Good, 2002; Rosenthal & Crisp, 2006; Good, Aronson, & Inzlicht, 2003;Johns, Schmader, & Martens, 2005; Martens, Johns, Greenberg, & Schimel, 2006)(but for exceptions outside the laboratory, see Cohen, Garcia, Apfel, & Master, 2006; Dasgupta & Asgari, 2004) and might prove important for future work on policy reform.

Schmader et al.'s (2008) Integrated Process model of stereotype threat is predicated on the idea that a state of disequilibrium lies at the root of a woman's susceptibility to stereotype threat effects – a state of dissonance between high math and gender identification in an environment that often embeds negative associations between these two identities (also see, Nosek, Banaji, and Greenwald, 2002). Women's colleges attempt to foster environmental cultures that refute gender-related stereotypes (Langdon, 2001). Hence, these institutions attempt to espouse positive associations between being a woman and excelling in math, which in turn, may promote a state of equilibrium between a woman's gender and math identification (also see Kawakami, J. Steele, Cifa, Phills, & Dovidio, 2008). This equilibrium in a single-gender schooling culture might be helpful in promoting resiliency to stereotype threat by maintaining and perhaps by even promoting high identification with both math and gender while relieving concerns about being viewed through the negative lens of a gender stereotype (C. Steele, 1997). This antidote – helping women to form positive associations between their gender and MSE domains – has been supported recently in the laboratory. Forbes and Schmader (2010) have shown that retraining women to form new positive automatic associations with the math domain helped to increase women's performance on a math test.

In a related line of work, Mendoza-Denton and colleagues (e.g., Mendoza-Denton, Downey, Purdie, Davis, & Pietrzak, 2002, Mendoza-Denton, Pietrzak, & Downey, 2008) have provided compelling evidence that students with a low level of Race-Based Rejection Sensitivity (RS-Race) and a high level of ethnic identity, maintained a higher level of academic performance longitudinally than peers who possessed both high levels of RS-Race and ethnic identification. A productive future direction, therefore, would be to explore women's gender-related rejection sensitivity in order to examine whether single-gender institutions draw individuals with and or promote lower levels of gender-related rejection sensitivity while concurrently encouraging high gender and math identification. This kind of investigation has the potential to integrate and to reconcile what have seemed to be disparate findings on the conditions under which high levels of group identification have been linked with stereotyped individuals' intact versus underperformance in domains alleging intellectual inferiority to their groups.

Furthermore, it is possible that the concept of gender itself might vary with regard to the degree to which it is essentialized and reified in single-gender versus coed institutions. In a recent evocative thought piece, Prentice and Miller (2007) argued that "all categories are not created equal in the minds' eye" (p. 202) based on work by Haslam and colleagues (e.g., Haslam, Rothschild, & Ernst, 2000), which showed that gender, ethnicity and race, emerged as the most highly psychologically essentialized human categories (e.g., Gelman, 2009; Medin & Ortony, 1989, Yzerbyt et al., 2001). Notably, Prentice and Miller argued that the extent to which a category is essentialized is intimately tied to social consequences such as stereotyping and motivation to correct performance (also see Prentice & Miller, 2006). Given this link between essentialism and stereotyping, it would be useful to examine the extent to which institutional variables as well as socially devalued individuals' levels of essentialist beliefs play a role in susceptibility versus resilience to phenomena such as stereotype threat. Furthermore, it would be of great value to explore the intersectionality of the aforementioned identities including socioeconomic status (see Cole, 2009; Gonzales, Blanton, & Williams, 2002), a moderately essentialized category (Haslam et al., 2000). Socioeconomic status is oftentimes a concealable stigma (see Quinn, Kahng, & Crocker, 2004) but it has nevertheless been implicated in stereotype threat effects in the United States (e.g., B. Spencer and Castano, 2007) in the face of a culture that purports to have more class mobility than it affords.

Despite the advances on understanding mediators and moderators of stereotype threat (e.g., Schmader et al., 2008), research on how to combat stereotype threat for women in MSE fields from a policy perspective is lacking. This reality is exacerbated by the fact that in coed environments, numerical representation serves to perpetuate threat in MSE cultures because it has been "explained" explicitly as resulting from a genetics theory of gender differences; an argument exemplified by Dr. Lawrence Summers', then president of Harvard University, comments in 2005 on the allegedly intrinsic nature of MSE women's "differential availability" at the high end of quantitative aptitude tests (Summers, 1/14/2005). In turn, a Summers-like biological explanation of gender differences has been shown to hinder women's math performance (Dar-Nimrod & Heine, 2006); and might continue to, especially if women in MSE fields remain mostly unaware of stereotype threat (see, Schmader, Johns, and Martens, 2004).

The main question concerning policy reform is how to best protect women from stereotype threat effects on an institutional level that removes this onus from women; who already bear the burden of negative stereotypes. The current work will hopefully spur further investigations outside the laboratory on protecting women from stereotype threat effects that would affect policy reform, such as exploring the impacts of creating single-gender MSE classrooms in coed settings (on the general advantages and disadvantages of this approach, see Cookston, 2009; Watterston, 2007). In the interim, it would be wise at the very least to hire more women faculty to teach MSE courses (see, Dasgupta & Asgari, 2004). In any case, it is crucial that policy reform would involve instructors, peers, allies, and women in MSE domains to foster positive associations between women and success in MSE careers, such that women could perform to their potential without having to sacrifice important aspects of their social identity and while placing more onus on institutions than on individuals to change environments to signal intellectual safety over threat.

References

Abrams, D. & Hogg, M. A. (1999). *Social identity and social cognition.* Malden, MA: Blackwell Publishers.

Alter, A. L., Aronson, J., Darley, J. M., Rodriguez, C., & Ruble, D. N. (2010). Rising to the threat: Reducing stereotype threat by reframing the threat as a challenge. *Journal of Experimental Social Psychology, 46,* 166-161.

Ambady, N., Paik, S. K., C. Steele, J., Owen-Smith, A., & Mitchell, J. P. (2004). Deflecting negative self-relevant stereotype activation: The effects of individuation. *Journal of Experimental Social Psychology, 40,* 401-408. doi: 10.1016/j.jesp.2003.08.003.

Aronson, J., Fried, C. B., & Good, C. (2002). Reducing the effects of stereotype threat on African American college students by shaping theories of intelligence. *Journal of Experimental Social Psychology, 38,* 113-125. doi: 10.1006/jesp.2001.1491.

Aronson, J., Lustina, M. J., Good, C., Keough, K., C. Steele, C. M., & Brown, J. (1999). When White men can't do math: Necessary and sufficient factors in stereotype threat. *Journal of Experimental Social Psychology, 35,* 29-46. doi: 10.1006/jesp.1998.1371.

Astin, H. S., & Sax, L. J. (1996). Undergraduate women in science: Personal and environmental influences on the development of scientific talent. In C. Davis, A. Ginorio, C. Hollenshead, B. Lazarus, & P. Rayman (Eds.), *The equity equation: Women in science, mathematics, and engineering* (pp. 96-121). San Francisco, CA: Jossey-Bass.

Brown, R. P., & Josephs, R. A. (1999). The mathematics identification questionnaire. The University of Texas at Austin, Unpublished manuscript.

Cohen, G. L., C. Steele, C. M., & Ross, L. D. (1999). The mentor's dilemma: Providing critical feedback across the racial divide. *Personality and Social Psychology Bulletin, 25,* 1302-1318.doi: 10.1177/0146167299258011.

Cohen, G. L., Garcia, J., Apfel, N., & Master, A. (2006). Reducing the racial achievement gap: A social-psychological intervention. *Science, 313,* 1307-1310.doi: 10.1126/science.1128317.

Cole, E. R. (2009). Intersectionality and research in Psychology. *American Psychologist,* 64, 170-180.doi: 10.1037/a0014564.

Cookston, P. W. (2009). Single-sex or coeducational classes. International Springer, 21, 919-927. doi: 10.1007/978-0-387-73317-3_60.

Dar-Nimrod, I., & Heine, S. J. (2006). Exposure to scientific theories affects women's math performance. *Science, 314,* 435.

Dasgupta, N., & Asgari, S. (2004). Seeing is believing: Exposure to counter stereotypic women leaders and its effect on automatic gender stereotyping. *Journal of Experimental Social Psychology,* 40, 642-658. doi:10.1016/j.jesp.2004.02.003.

Ekstrom, R. B., French, J. W., Harman, H., &Derman, D. (1976). *Kit of factor-referenced cognitive tests* (rev. ed.). Princeton, NJ: Educational Testing Service.

Forbes, C. E., &Schmader, T. (2010). Retraining attitudes and stereotypes to affect motivation and cognitive capacity under stereotype threat. *Journal of Personality and Social Psychology,* 99, 740-754.doi: 10.1037/a0020971

Gelman, S. A. (2009).Essentialist reasoning about the biological world. In A. Berthoz& Y. Christen (Eds.), *Neurobiology of "umwelt": How living beings perceive the world* (pp. 7-16). Berlin: Springer-Verlag.

Gonzales, P. M., Blanton, H., & Williams, K. J. (2002). The Effects of stereotype threat and double-minority status on the test performance of Latino women. *Personality and Social Psychology Bulletin, 28,* 659-670.

Good, C., Aronson, J., & Inzlicht, M. (2003). Improving adolescents' standardized test performance: An intervention to reduce the effects of stereotype threat. *Journal of Applied Developmental Psychology,* 24, 645-662. doi: 10.1016/j.appdev.2003.09.002.

Haslam, N., Rothschild, L., & Ernst, D. (2000). Essentialist beliefs about social categories. *British Journal of Social Psychology,* 39, 113-127. doi: 10.1348/014466600164363.

Huguet, P. & Régner, I. (2007). Stereotype threat among schoolgirls in quasi-ordinary classroom circumstances. *Journal of Educational Psychology, 99,* 545-560. doi: 10.1037/0022-0663.99.3.545.

Inzlicht, M., & Ben-Zeev, T. (2000). Do high-achieving female students underperform in private? The implications of threatening environments on intellectual processing. *Journal of Educational Psychology, 95,* 14-16.doi: 10.1037/0022-0663.95.4.796.

Inzlicht, M., & Ben-Zeev, T. (2003). Do high-achieving female students underperform in private? The implications of threatening environments on intellectual processing. *Journal of Educational Psychology, 95,* 796-805.doi: 10.1037/0022-0663.95.4.796.

Inzlicht, M., & Good, C. (2006). How environment can threaten academic performance, self-knowledge and sense of belonging. In S. Levin & C. van Laar (Eds.), *The Claremont symposium on applied social psychology* (pp.129-150). Mahwah, NJ, US: Lawrence Erlbaum Associates Publishers.

Jamieson, J.P., & Harkins, S.G. (2007). Mere effort and stereotype threat performance effects. *Journal of Personality and Social Psychology, 93,* 544-564.doi: 10.1037/0022-3514.93.4.544.

Johns, M., Schmader, T., & Martens, A. (2005). Knowing is half the battle: Teaching stereotype threat as a means of improving women's math performance. *Psychological Science, 16,* 175-179.doi: 10.1111/j.0956-7976.2005.00799.x.

Kawakami, K., Steele, J. R., Cifa, C., Phills, C. E., & Dovidio, J. F. (2008).Approaching math increases math =me and math = pleasant. *Journal of Experimental Social Psychology, 44,* 818-825.doi: 10.1016/j.jesp.2007.07.009.

Langdon, E. A. (2001). Women's colleges then and now: Access then, equity now. *Peabody Journal of Education, 76,* 5-30. Retrieved from http://www.jstor.org/stable/1493003.

Lirgg, C. D. (1994). Environmental perceptions of students in same-gender and coeducational physical education classes. *Journal of Educational Psychology, 86,* 183-92. doi: 10.1037/0022-0663.86.2.183.

Luhtanen, R., & Crocker, J. (1992). A collective self-esteem scale: Self-evaluation of one's social identity. *Personality and Social Psychology Bulletin, 18,* 302-318. doi: 10.1177/0146167292183006.

Major, B. N., & O'Brien, L. T. (2005).The social psychology of stigma. *Annual Review of Psychology, 56,* 393-421. doi: 10.1146/annurev.psych. 56.091103.070137.

Martens, A., Johns, M., Greenberg, J., & Schimel. (2006). Combating stereotype threat: The effect of self-affirmation on women's intellectual performance. *Journal of Experimental Social Psychology, 42,* 236-243.doi: 10.1016/ j.jesp.2005.04.010.

Marx, D. M., & Roman, J. S. (2002). Female role models: Protecting women's math test performance. *Personality and Social Psychology Bulletin, 28*, 1183-1193. doi: 0.1177/01461672022812004.

McIntyre, A. (2008). *Participatory action research*. Thousand Oaks, CA.: Sage Publications.

Medin, D., & Ortony, A. (1989). Psychological essentialism. In S. Vosniadou& A. Ortony (Eds.), *Similarity and analogical reasoning* (pp. 179–195). New York: Cambridge University Press.

Mendoza-Denton, R., Downey, G., Purdie, V., Davis, A., & Pietrzak, J. (2002) Sensitivity to status-based rejection: Implications for African American students' college experience. *Journal of Personality and Social Psychology, 83*, 896-918. doi: 10.1037/0022-3514.83.4.896.

Mendoza-Denton, R., Pietrzak, J., & Downey, G. (2008). Distinguishing institutional identification from academic goal pursuit: Interactive effects of ethnic identification and race-based rejection sensitivity. *Journal of Personality and Social Psychology, 95*, 338-351. doi: 10.1037/0022-3514.95.2.338.

Murphy, M. C., C. Steele, C. M., & Gross, J. J. (2007). Signaling threat: How situational cues affect women in math, science, and engineering settings. *Psychological Science, 10*, 879-885.doi: 10.1111/j.14679280.2007.01995.x.

Nosek, B. A., Banaji, M. R., & Greenwald, A. G. (2002). Math = male, me = female, therefore math ≠ me. *Journal of Personality and Social Psychology, 83*, 44-59.doi: 10.1037/0022-3514.83.1.44.

Prentice, D., & Miller, D. T. (2006). Essentializing differences between women and men. *Psychological Science, 17*, 129-135.doi: 10.1111/j.1467-9280.2006.01675.x.

Prentice, D., & Miller, D. T. (2007). Psychological essentialism of human categories. *Current Directions in Psychological Science, 16*, 202-206. doi: 10.1111/j.1467-8721.2007.00504.x.

Pronin, E., C. Steele, C. M., & Ross, L. (2004). Identity bifurcation in response to stereotype threat: women and mathematics. *Journal of Experimental Social Psychology, 40*, 152-164. doi: 10.1016/S0022-1031(03)00088-X.

Quinn, D. M., Kahng, S. K., & Crocker, J. (2004). Discreditable: Stigma effects of revealing a mental illness history on test performance. *Personality and Social Psychology Bulletin, 30*, 803-815. doi: 10.1177/0146167204264088.

Rosenthal, H. E. S., & Crisp, R. J. (2006). Reducing stereotype threat by blurring intergroup boundaries. *Personality and Social Psychology Bulletin, 32*, 501-511. doi: 10.1177/0146167205281009.

Schmader, T. (2002). Gender identification moderates stereotype threat effects on women's math performance. *Journal of Experimental Social Psychology, 38,* 194-201.doi: 10.1006/jesp.2001.1500.

Schmader, T., Johns, M., & Forbes, C. (2008).An integrated process model of stereotype threat effects on performance. *Psychological Review, 115,* 336-356. doi: 10.1037/0033-295X.115.2.336.

Sebrechts, J. S. (1992). Cultivating scientists at women's colleges. *Initiatives, 55,* 45-51.

Sekaquaptewa, D., and Thompson, M. (2003). Solo status, stereotypes, and performance expectancies: Their effects on women's public performance. *Journal of Experimental Social Psychology, 39,* 68-74.doi: 10.1016/S0022-1031(02)00508-5.

Shmurak, C. B. (1998).*Voices of hope: Adolescent girls at single sex and coeducational schools.* New York, NY: Peter Lang Publishing.

Spencer, B., & Castano, E. (2007). Social class is dead. Long live social class! Stereotype threat among low socioeconomic status individuals. *Social Justice Research, 20,* 418–432.

Steele, C. M. (1997). A threat in the air: How stereotypes shape intellectual identity and performance. *American Psychologist, 52,* 613-629. doi: 10.1037/0003-066X.52.6.613.

Steele, C. M., & Aronson, J. (1995). Stereotype threat and the intellectual test performance of African Americans. *Journal of Personality and Social Psychology, 69,* 797-811. doi: 10.1037/0022-3514.69.5.797.

Steele, C. M., Spencer, S. J., & Aronson, J. (2002). Contending with group image: The psychology of stereotype and social identity threat. In M. P. Zanna (Ed.), *Advances in experimental social psychology,* 379–440. Amsterdam: Academic Press.

Tajfel, H. & Turner, J. C. (1986). An integrative theory of intergroup conflict. In S. Worchel& W. Austin (Eds.), *Psychology of intergroup relations* (pp. 2-24). Chicago: Nelson-Hall.

Tidball, M. E., Smith, D. G., Tidball, C. S., & Wolf-Wendel, L. E. (Eds.). (1999). *Taking women seriously: Lessons and legacies for educating the majority.* Phoenix, AZ: Oryx Press.

Trickett, E.J., Trickett, P.K., Castro, J.J. and Schnaffner, P. (1982) The independent school experience: Aspects of the normative environments of single-gender and coed secondary schools. *Journal of Educational Psychology, 74,* 374–381. doi: 10.1037/0022-0663.74.3.374.

Walton, G. M., & Cohen, G. L. (2003). Stereotype lift. *Journal of Experimental Social Psychology, 39,* 456-467.

Yzerbyt V., Corneille, O., & Estrada C., 2001), The interplay of subjective essentialism and Entitativity in the formation of stereotypes. *Personality and Social Psychology Review,* 5, 141-155 doi: 0.1207/S15327957PSPR0502_5.

Yzerbyt, V., Muller, D., & Judd, C. M. (2004). Adjusting researchers' approach to adjustment: On the use of covariates when testing interactions. *Journal of Experimental Social Psychology,* 40, 42-431.doi: 10.1016/j.jesp.2003.10.001.

In: Psychology of Threat
Editors: B. Hunter and T. Romero

ISBN: 978-1-62257-344-8
© 2013 Nova Science Publishers, Inc.

Chapter 5

COGNITIVE SELF-REGULATION SKILLS AND THE BIG FIVE PERSONALITY TRAITS: A JOINT FACTOR ANALYSIS

*Tomoko Sugiura[1] and Yoshinori Sugiura[2,]**
[1]Japan Woman's University, Japan
[2]Hiroshima University, Japan

Abstract

The relationships between cognitive self-regulation skills and the Big Five personality traits were examined. Sugiura and Umaoka[2003] developed the Cognitive Self-Regulation Skills scale (CSRS) whose items were based on cognitive-behavioral therapy techniques.

The CSRS has two subscales: Logical Analysis and Refraining from Catastrophic Thinking. Examining the scale's relationship to personality traits was expected to provide useful clues to factors facilitating or inhibiting the use of cognitive self-regulation skills.

The CSRS and the Big Five Scale [Wada, 1996] were completed by 485 college students. A joint factor analysis revealed that the CSRS items were almost perfectly subsumed under the Big Five while retaining its two subscales. The items of Logical Analysis were included in Openness and the Refraining from Catastrophic Thinking items loaded negatively on Neuroticism. It is suggested that the intellectual and flexible style (Openness) supports the use of

* E-mail address: ysugiura@hiroshima-u.ac.jp; Tel: +81-82-424-6573; Fax: +81-82-424-0759; Address: Graduate School of Integrated Arts and Sciences, Hiroshima University, 1-7-1, Kagamiyama, Higashi-Hiroshima City, Hiroshima Prefecture, 739-8521, Japan. (Corresponding author)

active and objective problem-solving skills as measured by Logical Analysis, and that negative emotionality (Neuroticism) makes it difficult to be detached from negative thinking (the skills represented by Refraining from Catastrophic Thinking).

Keywords: Cognitive self-regulation skills, the Big Five, a joint factor analysis, cognitive-behavioral therapy

1. Introduction

Ample evidence has demonstrated that cognitive-behavioral therapy (CBT) is effective for various disorders [Chambliss and Ollendick, 2001]. CBT aims to foster adaptive cognitive self-regulation skills in distressed individuals. During therapy, patients learn, guided by therapists, how to cope adaptively with current and future problems [Freeman, Pretzer, Fleming, and Simon, 1990]. As the term "self-regulation" suggests, these skills are intended to be used voluntarily in daily life.

Some theories have proposed specific forms of adaptive cognitive self-regulation (e.g., social problem-solving skills [D'Zurilla, 1986] or metacognitive awareness [Teasdale et al., 2002]). In contrast, Sugiura and Umaoka[2003] developed the Cognitive Self-Regulation Skills scale (CSRS) to measure the voluntary use of more general CBT-like skills in daily life. The CSRS is a face-valid measure whose items are based on cognitive techniques used in CBT [Freeman, 1989; Freeman et al., 1990]. The CSRS has two factorially derived subscales, Logical Analysis (LA) and Refraining from Catastrophic Thinking (RCT). The former reflects active and objective problem-solving skills, while the latter measures the ability to be detached from negative thinking to alleviate catastrophic cognitions. A series of studies revealed its reliability and validity [Amari and Umaoka, 2002; Sugiura, Sugiura, and Umaoka, 2003; Sugiura and Umaoka, 2003]. This two-factor structure was validated by a confirmatory factor analysis. Both subscales of the CSRS evidenced good to acceptable internal consistency. Furthermore, LA was related to trait self-efficacy and a problem-focused coping style, which suggests that it reflects an active orientation towards problems. In contrast, RCT was negatively related to negative beliefs about intrusive thoughts [Cartwright-Hatton and Wells, 1997]. This suggests that RCT can alleviate negative thinking. By using structural equation modelling, Sugiura and Umaoka[2003] found that RCT reduced depressive symptoms among college students. LA had an indirect effect on depression by enhancing RCT. Sugiura and Sugiura[2003] confirmed the causal effect of RCT on depression by a longitudinal design.

Cognitive self-regulation skills are closely related to stress coping strategies in that both represent voluntarily adopted tactics. The difference is that the former is based on treatment techniques known to be effective, thus representing a normative approach, as opposed to the descriptive approach of the latter [D'Zurilla, 1986]. Sugiura et al. [2003] found that both CSRS subscales were related to positive interpretation, while LA was also related to problem-focused coping. These coping counterparts are often classified as adaptive [cf. Tobin, Holroyd, Reynolds, and Wigal, 1989], which supports the normative approach of the CSRS. However, the magnitudes of correlations were not very high (maximum $r = .51$), warranting the distinction between these constructs. Furthermore, RCT is conceptually unique due to its metacognitive focus [cf. Teasdale et al., 2002], i.e., it emphasizes how one relates to his/her own thinking.

In order to specify factors supporting the voluntary use of cognitive self-regulation skills, Sugiura et al. [2003] examined the relationship between the CSRS and the Big Five Scale [BFS; Wada, 1996]. The Big Five traits are the repeatedly found broader level factors of personality. John and Srivastava [1999] defined each dimension of the Big Five as follows. Extraversion is an energetic approach to the world. Agreeableness is a pro-social and communal orientation. Conscientiousness is socially prescribed impulse control. Neuroticism is negative emotionality. Openness represents the breadth, depth, originality, and complexity of mental and experiential life. Sugiura et al. [2003] conducted a partial correlation analysis controlling for each CSRS subscale and found that both CSRS subscales were correlated with Openness to experience. In addition, LA was correlated with Agreeableness, while RCT was negatively correlated with Neuroticism.

However, the stress-coping literature suggests caution when drawing firm conclusions about these relationships, especially regarding LA. The correlation between LA and Openness is consistent with studies that have found positive relationships between problem-focused coping and Openness [David and Suls, 1999; Heppner, Cook, Wright, and Johnson, 1995]. However, traits other than Openness have also been found to relate to problem-focused coping. David and Suls [1999] reviewed literature to find that problem-focused coping was related to Neuroticism, Extraversion, Agreeableness and Conscientiousness. Thus, every Big Five trait could be related to problem-focused coping. These findings might also hold true for LA, which is related to problem-focused coping [Sugiura et al., 2003].

Although multiple personality traits were found to be or could be related to cognitive self-regulation skills, how specific or robust are the relationships? Although cognitive self-regulation may correlate with multiple personality traits, it is possible that these relationships arise from methodological problems.

Multiple associations could be due to covariances among personality traits or the CSRS subscales. Although Sugiura et al. [2003] controlled for the covariance between the two CSRS subscales by a partial correlation analysis, they did not control for the correlations among the Big Five traits. It is also possible that the multiple relationships could be attributed to the heterogeneity of the CSRS subscales in relation to personality correlates. Analysis of individual items will address both of these issues. As the Big Five factors have been shown to be stable and robust [John and Srivastava, 1999], researchers have attempted to classify items tapping various constructs in relation to the Big Five by a joint factor analysis [e.g., Church, 1994; Ferguson, 2001].

This study reanalysed the data from Sugiura et al. [2003] combined with newly obtained data, using a joint factor analysis to further elucidate the relationships between cognitive self-regulation skills and the Big Five personality traits. Examining the scale's relationship to personality traits was expected to provide useful clues to factors facilitating or inhibiting the use of cognitive self-regulation skills.

Table 1. Simple Statistics and Internal Consistencies of All Variables ($N = 485$)

	M	SD	Internal consistency
Cognitive Self-Regulation Skills scale			
Logical Analysis	17.37	2.90	.76
Refraining from Catastrophic Thinking	12.25	2.97	.76
Big Five Scale			
Neutoticism	54.69	13.29	.92
Extraversion	54.63	13.04	.91
Openness	51.50	10.28	.86
Agreeableness	52.79	10.12	.84
Conscientiousness	46.13	9.89	.81

2. Method

2.1. Participants

Four hundred and eighty-five Japanese college students attending introductory psychology courses completed the questionnaires during class. The total sample consisted of 207 men and 278 women with a mean age of 19.48 years (SD = 1.40). Of 485 participants, 199 students appeared in Sugiura et al. [2003], while 286 participants were newly recruited for this study. They participated voluntarily or in exchange for a partial course credit. They were all free to omit the questionnaire. No students refused to complete the questionnaire.

2.2. Questionnaires

2.2.1. The Big Five Scale [BFS; Wada, 1996]

The BFS was developed to measure the Big Five personality traits, whose items are based on the Adjective Check List [ACL; Gough and Heilbrun, 1983]. A series of factor analyses of 198 theoretically selected ACL items resulted in the 60-item BFS. Each of the five factors contains 12 trait adjectives. Items were rated on a 7-point scale, 1(*not at all true*) to 7 (*very true*). Trait adjective approach has been known to be factorially robust [Wada, 1996]. Kashiwagi[1997] suggested that the ACL items(Japanese version), on which the BFS is based, could be theoretically classified under each of the five domains of the NEO PI-R [Costa and McCrae, 1992], the most widely used measure of the Big Five.

2.2.2. The Cognitive Self-Regulation Skills Scale[CSRS; Sugiura and Umaoka, 2003]

The CSRS has two subscales. LA has six items and RCT has five items (see Table 2). Participants were asked the extent to which they thought they could do things described in each item when they were anxious. They responded on a 4-point scale, 1(*absolutely I cannot*) to 4 (*surely I can*).

3. Results

Means, standard deviations and alpha reliability coefficients of all scales are shown in Table 1. All scales exhibited acceptable to excellent reliability (α = .76 -.91).

Sixty BFS items and 11 CSRS items were jointly factor analysed. We followed Wada's [1996] factor analysis procedure for our data. Iterated principal factor analysis with promax rotation was conducted. In order to help items distribute evenly among factors, equamax was was chosen as the prerotation method. When the itemsincrease, the varimax rotation tends to yield an overly heavy first factor. Oblique rotation was chosen because significant, albeit weak, correlations have been repeatedly found among the Big Five factors [John and Srivastava, 1999]. A factor pattern instead of a factor structure was examined in order to clarify the unique contributions of each factor to each item (controlling for other factors). A scree plot suggested around five factors. Thus, five factors were extracted on a theoretical basis, accounting for 41% of the total variance[1].

Table 2 shows the factor pattern of the joint factor analysis. Interfactor correlations are also shown in Table 2. The Big Five factors were almost perfectly replicated. All LA items positively loaded on Openness (all loadings greater than .37), while all RCT items negatively loaded on Neuroticism (the absolute values of all loadings greater than |.29|). None of the LA items had loadings greater than |.30| on factors other than Openness. As for RCT, only one item, "Even in such a situation, I keep bright hope and think that I can change adversities into benefit." also loaded on Openness (.41). Weak interfactor correlations were observed. The mean of absolute interfactor correlations was |.18|, which was somewhat smaller than |.21| of Wada [1996]. In sum, the joint factor analysis yielded a very clear five-factor solution, under which the CSRS items are classified while retaining its original two subscales.

4. Discussion

This study conducted a joint factor analysis on the Big Five and cognitive self-regulation skills in order to clarify the relationships between these constructs on the level of individual items. Cognitive self-regulation skills were almost perfectly subsumed under the Big Five personality structure, while retaining its two subcategories. This suggests the Big Five traits offer a useful framework for understanding the function of cognitive self-regulation. Factorial stability of the CSRS subscales was reported by Sugiura et al. [2003] and Sugiura and Umaoka [2003]. This study lends further support for the distinction between and the homogeneity within the two CSRS subscales by showing that the two correspond to different personality traits.

---

[1]Two to eight factor solutions were tried for comparison. With four or fewer factors, some of the Big Five factors (e.g., E and O or A and C) merged. With six factors, Logical Analysis formed an independent factor; with more factors, A or O split.

Table 2. Results of a Joint Factor Analysis of the Big Five and Cognitive Self-Regulation Skills (N = 485)

Items	N	E	O	A	C
N: ruminating[a].	87				
N: anxious.	81				
N: worrying.	78				
N: feelings easily hurt.	75				
N: whiny.	73				
N: tired from worrying.	66				
N: feelings easily upset.	65				
N: pessimistic.	64				
N: depressive.	59				
N: nervous.	52				
N: tense.	50				
Even if the bad consequences of the problem come to my mind, I can reassure myself that they are nothing more than my imagination.[b]	-29				
When I start thinking about the situation seriously, I can stop it for a while.	-41				
Even in such a situation, I keep bright hope and think that I can change adversity into benefit.	-44		41		
Even though I do not feel good, I don't think catastrophically.	-47				
I don't develop a bad scenario from the situation.	-47				
N: not lose sleep over worries, resilient.	-69				
E: talkative.		77			
E: cheerful.		77			
E: gregarious.		71			
E: outgoing.		68			
E: has positive attitude.		64			
E: active.		60			
E: modest.		-58			
E: inhibited.		-60			
E: unsociable.		-64			
E: joyless.		-70			
E: sulky.		-71			

Table 2. Continued

Items	N	E	O	A	C
E: silent.		-80			
O: untraditional.			61		
O: imaginative.			61		
O: inventive.			58		
O: versatile.			56		
O: insightful.			56		
O: ingenious.			53		
O: curious.			52		
O: broad-interests.			49		
I can consider both good and bad aspects of the situation and will be able to search for possible actions.			48		
I can think of several alternatives about how to think or how to act.			47		
O: artistic.			46		
O: talented.			45		
I can quietly consider the meaning of the problem to myself.			43		
O: independent.			42		
O: intelligent.			42		
I reflect on my habitual ways of conceiving or seeing situations.			39		
I can think of several reasons which caused this problem.			37		
I imagine solving a problem.			37		
A: impatient.				.74	
A: irritable.				.73	
A: rebellious.				.61	
A: temperamental.				.58	
A: selfish.				.55	
A: critical.				.53	
C: unscrupulous.				.35	
A: compliant.				-.31	
A: cooperative.				-.40	
A: kind.			37	-.42	

Table 2. Continued

Items	N	E	O	A	C
A: conscientious[c].			31	-.45	
A: forgiving.			33	-.48	
A: gentle.				-.69	
C: unreliable.					71
C: careless.					71
C: lazy.					56
C: unplanful.					52
C: untidy.					52
C: lack of attention to details.					44
C: hasty.				.34	40
C: fickle.					38
C: industrious.				34	-35
C: precise.					-46
C: deliberate.					-56
		N	E	O	A	C
		N	E	O	A	C
Interfactor correlations.	N	1.00	-27	-12	25	10
	E		1.00	31	-26	-08
	O			1.00	-14	01
	A				1.00	21
	C					1.00

Note. The rotated factor pattern of promax rotation is shown. Loadings greater than $|.30|$ are depicted. The exception is one CSRS item, "Even if the bad consequences of the problem come to my mind, I can reassure myself that they are nothing more than my imagination.", which had no loading greater than $|.30|$ on any of the five factors.

[a]For the BFS (the Big Five Scale), currently available English translations of items by John and Wada [S. Wada, personal communication, March 26, 2003] are shown. Alphabets before items indicate the initials of the Big Five factors on which they originally loaded in Wada [1996]. N = Neuroticism; E = Extraversion; O = Openness; A = Agreeableness; C = Conscientiousness.

[b]For the CSRS (the Cognitive Self-Regulation Skills scale), English translations of items made for this study are given in italics.

[c]Although "conscientious" loading on Agreeableness, not on Conscientiousness, may seem contradictory, it is not a mistake. Wada [1996] suggested that in the Eastern countries such as Japan, the distinction between intrapersonal and interpersonal characteristics might be somewhat obscure.

It should be emphasized that the present findings do not undermine the uniqueness of the CSRS. Because the Big Five traits are the highest order superfactors of personality [John and Srivastava, 1999], more specific and concrete measurements are needed depending on the purpose of the research. McCrae and Costa [1996, 1999] introduced the five-factor theory personality system, a multi-component model of personality, in which basic tendencies and characteristic adaptations were distinguished. Basic tendencies are deep and stable psychological structures. The Big Five traits are the constructs at this level. Characteristic adaptations are patterns of thoughts, feelings and behaviors individuals develop according to their personality traits. Although the term characteristic implies relatively enduring styles, they can change over time. This is in contrast to basic tendencies. Cognitive self-regulation skills correspond to characteristic adaptations.

As such, they are affected by personality traits [Neuroticism and Openness], but could be changed by interventions. Hereafter, the specific relationships found in the joint factor analysis are considered.

Logical Analysis (LA) was included in Openness. This suggests that the intellectual and flexible style supports the use of logical problem-solving skills. The previous report [Sugiura et al., 2003] found that LA was also related to Agreeableness. However, the more stringent method of the joint factor analysis revealed that the most important factor behind LA was Openness. Miller [1991] suggested that Openness facilitated responsiveness to psychotherapy. Perhaps, Openness may be most relevant to CBT on which the CSRS items are based. Beck, Rush, Shaw, and Emery[1979] conceptualized their therapy as corroborative research by therapists and patients. In CBT, patients are required, for example, to systematically record and examine their beliefs, and test their validity empirically in behavioral experiments [Wells, 1997]. Clearly, these processes will be facilitated by intellect, curiosity, or flexibility, the very characteristics of Openness. In addition, open people are characterized by the need for experiences that would provide incentive to tolerate ambiguity and dissonance [McCrae and Costa, 1997]. With openness, people would dare to examine their beliefs. The logical and scientific nature of CBT strategies is represented by LA [Sugiura et al., 2003]. Even more emphasis is placed on rational and systematic problem-solving skills in problem-solving therapy [D'Zurilla, 1986]. Thus, Openness is expected to predict the response to problem-solving therapy.

Refraining from Catastrophic Thinking (RCT) loaded negatively on Neuroticism. Many emotional disorders are characterized by negative and relatively uncontrollable thoughts [Wells and Matthews, 1994]. In other words, those with emotional disorders cannot detach themselves from negative thinking. Needless to say, Neuroticism has been repeatedly shown to be a vulnerability factor to many emotional disorders [e.g., Hirshfeld and Klerman, 1979; Widiger, Verheul, and van den Brink, 1999]. Thus, it is natural that Neuroticism should make it difficult to be detached from negative thinking. In the field of coping research, detached coping is a relatively new construct [Roger, Jarvis, and Najarian, 1993]. Thus, the finding on the relationship between RCT and Neuroticism would increase the accumulating evidence.

RCT reduces depressive symptoms [Sugiura and Sugiura, 2003; Sugiura and Umaoka, 2003]. Although this is seemingly consistent with the negative relationship between RCT and Neuroticism, inferring causality between these two variables requires caution. As personality traits are stable structures [McCrae and Costa, 1996, 1999], it is conceptually unlikely that cognitive self-regulation skills reduce Neuroticism. Empirical findings also support this point. Teasdale and Dent [1987] found that even after recovery, depressive patients' cognitive biases did not totally disappear, but only became inactive. Recovered patients' negative cognitive processing is activated again when they are in a negative mood. This dormant vulnerability may explain the high relapse rates of depression [Segal, Williams, and Teasdale, 2002]. Teasdale and Dent [1987] also found that depressive cognitive biases were associated with Neuroticism. Considering the findings on persistent vulnerability, the relationship between RCT and Neuroticism cannot be interpreted as the former reducing the latter. Within the design of this study, it is safe to conclude that Neuroticism had an inhibiting effect on RCT. This suggests that the depression-reducing effect of cognitive self-regulation skills requires a different explanation from that for the personality effect. RCT may moderate the toxic influences of Neuroticism. Segal et al. [2002] developed an intervention called Mindfulness-Based Cognitive Therapy (MBCT) for depression.MBCT aims to foster metacognitive awareness, which is defined as "a cognitive set in which negative thoughts and feelings are seen as passing mental events rather than as aspects of self" (p. 275). With metacognitive awareness, even if depressive cognitive biases give rise to negative thoughts, one can be detached from them. RCT and metacognitive awareness are functionally similar in that both prevent individuals from becoming overly involved in their thinking.

In sum, this study clarified the specific relationships between the subcategories of cognitive self-regulation skills and the Big Five personality traits. Some clinical implications can be extracted from the present results. People who are open to experience are expected to respond well to CBT. More initiative may be assigned to these patients, such as requesting them to use self-help books. On the other hand, those with low openness require the therapist to be more active.

Considerable time and effort will be needed for socialization [Wells, 1997], in which therapists educate patients about CBT and share the cognitive case formulation with them. When patients can experience the relief of distress using cognitive strategies during the first session, their engagement in treatment will be enhanced [Beck et al., 1979]. People high in Neuroticism will constantly experience negative emotions and are expected to have difficulty detaching themselves from negative thoughts. In order to help them, using behavioral techniques such as activity scheduling to improve their mood would be useful [Beck et al., 1979; Freeman et al., 1990]. The more active they become using these techniques, the more satisfaction they will have, improving their emotional states. At this point, cognitive techniques could be successfully introduced. Although these techniques are not novel, the present findings suggest the utility of self-report measures to predict the therapy process.

The limitations of the present study and future directions should also be noted. First, the study must be replicated with diverse populations. Second, examining the relationships with various facets of the Big Five would be informative. The Big Five traits are superfactors that include several facets (subscales). The NEO PI-R [Costa and McCrae, 1992] has six facets under each of the Big Five factors (domains). For example, Openness has facets such as Ideas, Fantasy, Aesthetics, Actions, Feelings, and Values. Which of these six are most relevant to LA? This type of investigation is difficult with the BFS, which does not include facets. Finally, conducting similar analyses on constructs related to cognitive self-regulation, for example self-efficacy, optimism, or social problem-solving skills, is important for the purpose of comparison. Hopefully, findings from the questionnaire studies of self-regulation and the clinical practice of CBT will influence each other.

Acknowledgments

This research was supported by a grant from the Japan Society for the Promotion of Science. We thank Sayuri Wada for providing the English translation of the Big Five Scale.

References

Aamri, T., and Umaoka, K. (2002). Nintitekitousei to jikokoryoku-kangajyosidaigakusei no yokuutu to fuannioyobosueikyo [Effects of cognitive control and self-efficacy on depression and anxiety in female university students]. *Journal of the Graduate School: Home Economics, Human Life Sciences*, 8, 29-39.

Beck, A. T., Rush, A. J., Shaw, B. F., and Emery, G. (1979). *Cognitive therapy of depression*. New York: Guilford Press.

Cartwright-Hatton, S., and Wells, A. (1997). Beliefs about worry and intrusions: The meta-cognitions questionnaire and its correlates. *Journal of Anxiety Disorders*, 11, 279-296.

Chambless, D. L., and Ollendick, T. H. (2001). Empirically supported psychological interventions: Controversies and evidence. *Annual Review of Psychology*, 52, 685-716.

Church, A. T. (1994). Relating the Tellegen and five-factor models of personality structure. *Journal of Personality and Social Psychology*, 67, 898-909.

Costa, P. T., Jr., and McCrae, R. R. (1992).*NEO PI-R professional manual*. Odessa, F. L.: Psychological Assessment Resources.

David, J. P., and Suls, J. (1999). Coping efforts in daily life: Role of Big Five traits and problem appraisals. *Journal of Personality*, 67, 265-294.

D'Zurilla, T. J. (1986). *Problem-Solving Therapy: A social competence approach to clinical intervention*. New York: Springer Publishing Company.

Ferguson, E. (2001). Personality and coping traits: A joint factor analysis. *British Journal of Health Psychology*, 6, 311-325.

Freeman, A. (1989). *Nintiryohonyumon* [The practice of cognitive therapy].(Y. Yusa et al., trans.). Tokyo: SeiwaShoten.

Freeman, A., Pretzer, J., Fleming, B., and Simon, K. M. (1990). *Clinical applications of cognitive therapy*. New York: Prenum Press.

Gough, H. G., and Heilbrun, A. B. (1983). *The adjective check list manual* (1983 ed). Palo Alto, C. A.: Consulting Psychologist Press.

Heppner, P. P., Cook, S. W., Wright, D. M., and Johnson, W. C., Jr. (1995). Progress in resolving problems: A problem-focused style of coping. *Journal of Counseling Psychology*, 42, 279-293.

Hirschfeld, R., and Klerman, G. (1979). Personality attributes and affective disorders. *American Journal of Psychiatry*, 136, 67-70.

John, O. P., and Srivastava, S. (1999). The Big Five trait taxonomy: History, measurement, and theoretical perspectives. In L. A. Pervin and O. P. John (Eds.), *Handbook of personality* (2nd ed., pp. 102-138.). New York: Guilford.

Kashiwagi, S. (1997).*Seikaku no hyouka to hyougen: Tokusei go insi-ronkara no approach* [Evaluation and representation of personality: Big Five traits approach]. Tokyo: Yuhikaku.

McCrae, R. R., and Costa, P. T., Jr. (1996). Toward a new generation of personality theories: Theoretical contexts for the five-factor model. In J. S. Wiggins (Ed.), *The five-factor model of personality: Theoretical perspectives*(pp. 51-87). New York: Guilford.

McCrae, R. R., and Costa, P. T., Jr. (1997). Conceptions and correlates of openness to experience. In R. Hogan, J. Johnson, and S. Briggs (Eds.), *Handbook of personality psychology*(pp. 825-847). San Diego, C. A.: Academic Press.

McCrae, R. R., and Costa, P. T., Jr. (1999). A five-factor theory of personality. In L. A. Pervin and O. R. John (Eds.), *Handbook of personality* (2nd ed., pp. 139-153). New York: Guilford.

Miller, T. R. (1991). The psychotherapeutic utility of the five-factor model of personality: A clinician's experience. *Journal of Personality Assessment, 57,* 415-433.

Roger, D., Jarvis, G., and Najarian, B. (1993). Detachment and coping: the construction and validation of a new scale for measuring coping strategies. *Personality and Individual Differences, 15,* 619-626.

Segal, Z. V., Williams, J. M. G., and Teasdale, J. D. (2002). *Mindfulness-Based Cognitive Therapy for depression.* New York: Guilford.

Sugiura, T., and Sugiura, Y. (2003).Nintitekitousei no sutoresukanwakoka: Yokuutu to no kanren [Stress buffering effect of cognitive-control: A moderator of stressor effect on depression]. *The Japanese Journal of Personality, 12,* 34-35.

Sugiura, T., Sugiura, Y., and Umaoka, K. (2003).Nintitekitousei to kanrensuruyouin: Seikakutokusei, meta-ninti to taisho style [Correlates of cognitive control: Personality traits, meta-cognitions, and coping styles]. *Journal of the Graduate School: Home Economics, Human Life Sciences, 9,* 13-23.

Sugiura, T., and Umaoka, K. (2003).Jyosidaigakuseiniokerunintitekitousei to yokuutu to no kanren[The relationship between Cognitive Control and depression in female university students]. *Japanese Journal of Health Psychology, 16,* 31-42.

Teasdale, J. D., and Dent, J. (1987). Cognitive vulnerability to depression: An investigation of two hypothesis. *British Journal of Clinical psychology, 26,* 113-126.

Teasdale, J. D., Moore, R. G., Hayhurst, H., Pope, M., Williams, S., and Segal, Z. V. (2002). Metacognitive awareness and prevention of relapse in depression: Empirical evidence. *Journal of Consulting and Clinical psychology, 70,* 275-287.

Tobin, D.L., Holroyd, K.A., Reynolds, R.V., and Wigal, J.K. (1989). The hierarchical factor structure of the Coping Strategies Inventory. *Cognitive Therapy and Research*, 13, 343-361.

Wada, S. (1996). Seikaku-tokuseigowomotiita Big Five shakudo no sakusei[Construction of the Big Five scales of personality trait terms and concurrent validity with N. P. I.]. *The Japanese Journal of Psychology*, 67, 61-67.

Wells, A. (1997). *Cognitive therapy of anxiety disorders*. Chichester, U. K.: John Wiley.

Wells, A., and Matthews, G. (1994). *Attention and emotion*. Hove, U.K.: Laurence Erlbaum Associates.

Widiger, T. A., Verheul, R., and van den Brink, W. (1999). Personality and psychopathology. In L. A. Pervin and O. R. John (Eds.), *Handbook of personality* (2nd ed., pp. 347-366). New York: Guilford.

In: Psychology of Threat   ISBN: 978-1-62257-344-8
Editors: B. Hunter and T. Romero   © 2013 Nova Science Publishers, Inc.

Chapter 6

MEASURING THREAT AS IT RELATES TO SOCIAL POLICY: PSYCHOMETRIC CONSIDERATIONS

James P. Clifton[1]* *and Christopher L. Aberson*[2]
[1]University of California, Merced, CA, US
[2]Humboldt State University, CA, US

Abstract

Intergroup threat theory (ITT) holds that different types of threats promote negative attitudes directed toward outgroups (e.g., Stephan and Stephan 2000). ITT shows predictive power in a wide variety of intergroup contexts (Stephan and Stephan 2000), such as: attitudes between Whites and Blacks (Aberson and Gaffney 2009), attitudes between Mexicans and Americans (Stephan, Diaz-Loving, and Duran 2000), and women's attitudes toward men (Stephan et al. 2000). The present chapter applies ITTs focus on threat to prediction of attitudes toward social policies with a particular focus on attitudes toward same-sex marriage. We propose that opposition to social policies arise from perceived threats associated with the implementation of those policies. Therefore, perceived threats are central to the understanding of policy attitudes, and the measurement of perceived threats as they relate to social policy is arguably of considerable importance in explaining policy attitudes. Using the example of attitudes toward same-sex marriage ($n = 263$),

*E-mail address: jclifton@ucmerced.edu

we demonstrate how (a) creating an item pool representative of relevant threat domains, (b) using both exploratory and confirmatory factor analytic procedures to address the psychometric properties of threat scales, and (c) using factor analytic evidence in conjunction with a qualitative analysis of item content to decide on the most appropriate selection of items were utilized to create distinct measures of threat.

PACS 05.45-a, 52.35.Mw, 96.50.Fm

Keywords: intergroup threat theory, realistic threat, symbolic threat, same-sex marriage

AMS Subject Classification: 53D, 37C, 65P

1. Introduction

Accurate identification and measurement of perceived threats as they relate to social policy is of considerable importance in explaining policy attitudes (Bobo and Tuan 2006), yet the process of measuring such threat is not always straightforward. Political-psychological debates are nested within a broader level of analysis encompassing political, geographical, historical, and economic contexts (Durrheim et al. 2009; Tetlock 2007), so it is important to consider contextual factors when measuring threat perceptions. In line with intergroup threat theory (ITT), we argue that perceptions of threat give rise to policy opposition, and that researchers must understand how these threats operate within a broader social milieu (Stephan, Ybarra, and Morrison 2009).

Using the framework of ITT, this chapter focuses on the creation of threat measures as they relate to social policy, using an example of attitudes toward same-sex marriage. Additionally, this chapter explores the validity of distinguishing between a refined causal explanation (i.e., realistic and symbolic threats) and a simple causal description (e.g., collective threat) of policy attitudes as a function of contextually relevant factors. The process for creating threat measures outlined in this chapter consists of identifying relevant threats vis-à-vis the policy of interest, which may be derived from empirical literature and media resources, conducting an item analysis to determine the relative fit of threat items, and using exploratory and confirmatory factor analytic procedures to analyze item structure.

In the following section, we describe the progression of threat research relevant to ITT. Types of threat may come from real sources (e.g., war between neighboring countries), symbolic sources (e.g., differing cultural beliefs), may be based on inaccurate perceptions (e.g., endorsement of outgroup stereotypes), and may concern individuals' apprehensions about intergroup interaction (e.g., when contact with an outgroup provokes feelings of anxiety).

1.1.   Realistic Threat

Early research on the types of threat that lead to hostile or antagonistic outgroup attitudes is based in realistic group conflict theory (RGCT). RGCT states that a real conflict of group interests, such as competition between groups for scarce resources, results in negative outgroup attitudes (LeVine and Campbell 1972; Sherif 1966). Sources of real threat do not have to involve competition over scarce resources, and may instead entail threats to ingroup welfare, such as threats posed to the economic or political power of the ingroup (LeVine and Campbell 1972), as well as material threats to individuals (e.g., when economic problems result in job loss). Furthermore, what a person thinks or feels is threatening is more important than reality (Bobo 1983). In other words, people need not base their attitudes on whether a threat truly exists, only that it is perceived as such. For instance, the proportion of immigrants perceived to live in close proximity to an ingroup is a more important predictor of exclusionary attitudes than the actual number of immigrants who live close (Pettigrew, Wagner, and Christ 2010; Semyonov et al. 2004).

1.2.   Symbolic Threat

Symbolic beliefs may cause negative intergroup attitudes, even in the absence of competition or conflicting goals (Sears 1988). Symbolic racism theory suggests that antiblack affect, traditional values, and the values of equality and individualism deeply rooted in American culture may be used to justify prejudice and discrimination (Kinder and Sears 1981; McConahay 1983; Sears 1988). The relationship between symbolic racism and positions on issues such as racial policy, busing, affirmative action, and welfare, even after controlling for factors such as political ideology and party identification is widely supported (Kinder and Sears 1981; Kluegel and Smith 1983; McConahay and Hough 1976; Sears and Allen 1984; Sears and Citrin 1985; Sears and Kinder 1993). For example, Whites may believe that policies such as affirmative action and welfare provide an unjust advantage to Blacks because they violate the American value of equality (Sawires and Peacock 2000). Symbolic racism theory also posits that differences in values are grounds for prejudice (Kinder and Sears 1981; McConahay 1983). For instance, Whites evaluate Blacks more negatively when they believe that Blacks do not support their system of values (Biernat, Vescio, and Theno 1996). Aspects of symbolic racism theory appear relevant to attitudes toward other types of outgroups as well. For example, attitudes toward homosexuals are more negative when heterosexuals perceive that the two groups have dissimilar values (Haddock, Zanna, and Esses 2008).

1.3. Intergroup Anxiety

Apart from realistic and symbolic sources of threat, apprehensions about interacting with outgroup members also promote negative outgroup attitudes (Stephan and Stephan 2000). This construct, called intergroup anxiety, is qualitatively different from realistic and symbolic threats, which depend on historical context (Stephan, Ybarra, and Morrison 2009). Intergroup anxiety may arise because a person fears negative evaluations by members of an outgroup (Stephan and Stephan 1985). For instance, external pressures (e.g., fear of social disapproval) to respond in an unbiased manner may result in heightened anxiety during intergroup contact (Trawalter, Richeson, and Shelton 2009). In contemporary America, there is a strong positive regard for equality in political, economic, social, and civil rights (Gaertner and Dovidio 1986). For individuals who strongly endorse egalitarianism, it may be important to control any underlying prejudices that they hold with respect to stigmatized groups. Consequently, they may worry about being perceived as prejudiced during intergroup contact, promoting feelings of anxiety and discomfort (Crocker, Major, and Steele 1998; Gaertner and Dovidio 1986; Stephan and Stephan 1985). Trying to control this anxiety depletes cognitive resources during intergroup contact (Richeson and Trawalter 2005), leading to biased processing of information and amplified emotional responses, which may in turn promote more negative outgroup attitudes (Stephan & Stephan, 1985).

2. Intergroup Threat Theory

Early research on realistic and symbolic threat pitted them in competition with one another (Sniderman and Tetlock 1986). Other work suggests both are important in predicting attitudes toward outgroups (e.g., Stephan, Ybarra, and Bachman 1999). More recently, researchers have raised concerns over whether it is important to distinguish between realistic and symbolic threat given that they often strongly overlap (Durrheim et al. 2009; Riek et al. 2010). We argue that some social contexts do not warrant a distinction between the two, for reasons we explain later. However, they are theoretically distinct constructs, and in many situations, symbolic threat predicts attitudes in manners that realistic threat does not. Similarly, realistic threat may predict aspects of attitudes that symbolic threat does not (Riek, Mania, and Gaertner 2006). For example, both symbolic and realistic aspects of prejudice are distinctively tied to opposition to bilingual education (Huddy and Sears 2008; Sears and Huddy 1993). Thus, state of the art threat research has shifted from a focus on competing theories into a single unifying theory, called intergroup threat theory (formerly titled integrated threat theory; Stephan and Stephan 2000; Stephan, Ybarra, and Morrison 2009).

Intergroup threat theory distinguishes between two broad classes of threat perception: realistic threats and symbolic threats, which may be further reduced into individuals and group components (Stephan, Ybarra, and Morrison 2009). Realistic threat may be broadly defined as threats to ingroup or individual welfare; symbolic threat by perceptions of differing worldviews. In other words, the former may be thought of as tangible or material threats and the latter as abstract and symbolic.

The major premise of ITT is that negative attitudes arise out of perceptions of threat. Importantly, ITT places an emphasis on understanding the context of intergroup relations to identify the most salient predictors of intergroup attitudes, because threat-attitude relationships and threat content depend upon the groups examined (Kamans et al. 2010; Riek, Mania, and Gaertner 2006; Stephan, Ybarra, and Morrison 2009). For example, low power groups (e.g., ethnic or sexual minorities) possess fewer resources than high power groups and therefore react differently to perceptions of threat than high power groups (Johnson, Terry, and Louis 2008; Kamans et al. 2010). As a result, the relationship between threats and attitudes is different for low power groups and high power groups.

The four main categories of threat in ITT are realistic group threat, symbolic group threat, realistic individual threat, and symbolic individual threat. Intergroup anxiety is considered a subtype of threat influenced by situational factors. Although ITT makes a fine distinction between individual and collective threat, collective threat holds primacy in social policy contexts because opposition to social transformation policies arises largely from perceived threats to the majority group's dominant position (Bobo and Hutchings 1996). Thus, the present chapter's focus is primarily on collective (group) threat, as are the threat items included in our motivating example. In the following sections, we define these threats as they relate specifically to ITT.

2.0.1. Realistic threat

Based on realistic group conflict theory (LeVine and Campbell 1972; Sherif 1966), and research showing that perceived threat is a more important predictor of attitudes than actual threat (e.g., Bobo 1983), ITT defines realistic threat as perceived threats to ingroup welfare or safety, as well as perceived threats to economic and political power (Stephan, Ybarra, and Morrison 2009). For example, in studies examining attitudes toward African Americans, realistic threat addresses issues such as "Blacks dominate American politics more than they should," and "Too much money is spent on educational programs that benefit Blacks (e.g., Stephan et al. 2002)." Similarly, in a study examining attitudes toward affirmative action, realistic threat addressed issues such as "Affirmative action leads to costly lawsuits that hurt American businesses," and "Affirmative action fosters hostility and violence directed at the majority group (Renfro et al. 2006)."

2.0.2. Symbolic threat

Attitudes based on theories of symbolic racism are known as symbolic threat (e.g., Sears 1988), defined in ITT as threats to morals, values, beliefs, and traditions of an ingroup (Esses, Haddock, and Zanna 1993; Stephan and Stephan 2000). For example, in studies examining attitudes toward African Americans, symbolic threat addresses issues such as "Whites and Blacks have very different values," and "Blacks want their rights to be put ahead of the rights of Whites (e.g., Stephan et al. 2002);" and in a study examining attitudes toward affirmative action, symbolic threat addressed issues such as "Affirmative action is wrong because it is an attempt to legislate morality," and "The kind of people who benefit from affirmative action have the same work values as the majority of Americans (reverse-scored; Renfro et al. 2006)."

2.0.3. Intergroup anxiety

Intergroup anxiety is a threat centered on feelings of anxiety or discomfort during interaction (or anticipated interaction) with an outgroup. It may result in various negative affective, cognitive, and behavioral consequences (Stephan and Stephan 1985). Intergroup anxiety is a strong predictor in ITT models and often demonstrates a stronger relationship with intergroup attitudes than either realistic or symbolic threat (Riek, Mania, and Gaertner 2006). For example, the intergroup anxiety scale asks participants how anxious (apprehensive, nervous, etc.) they would feel when interacting with members of the relevant outgroup on a 10-point scale ranging from (*not at all*) to (*extremely*).

3. Applications of ITT

Intergroup threat theory is particularly good at explaining the relationship between threats and attitudes (Riek, Mania, and Gaertner 2006), including attitudes toward social transformation policies such as affirmative action (Renfro et al. 2006) and Black Economic Empowerment policies in South Africa (Durrheim et al. 2009). The predictive power of ITT has been demonstrated in a variety of intergroup contexts (Stephan and Stephan 2000), such as: attitudes between Whites and Blacks (Aberson and Gaffney 2009; Riek et al. 2010); attitudes between Whites and Native Canadians (Corenblum and Stephan 2001); attitudes between Mexicans and Americans (Stephan, Diaz-Loving, and Duran 2000); and women's attitudes toward men (Stephan et al. 2000). Intergroup threat theory has also been used to explain attitudes toward immigrants (Bizman and Yinon 2001; Curseu, Stoop, and Schalk 2007; Kauff and Wagner 2012; Leong and Ward 2011; Matera, Stefanile, and Brown 2011; Rohmann, Florack, and Piontkowski 2006; Schweitzer et al. 2005; Stephan et al. 1998; Stephan, Ybarra, and Bachman 1999; Stephan et al. 2005) and international students (Charles-Toussaint and Crowson 2010); individuals with stigmatizing conditions, such as cancer or AIDS (Berrenberg et al. 2002); religious groups (González et al. 2008; Tausch, Hewstone, and Roy 2009); political parties (Osborne, Davies, and Duran 2008; Riek et al. 2010); and social policies (Durrheim et al. 2009; Renfro et al. 2006; Sibley and Liu 2004).

3.1. ITT Applied to Same-Sex Marriage

The literature on same-sex marriage is replete with reasons why people oppose same-sex marriage, many of which fall into the categories of realistic or symbolic threat. For instance, the belief that same-sex marriage violates traditional values of gender and family (Price, Nir, and Cappella 2005) is a symbolic threat, and the belief that same-sex marriage will result in tax increases (Stivers and Valls 2007) or that children raised by same-sex parents are at risk for developmental problems (Patterson 2006) fall under the domain of realistic threat. In addition, several theories posit that anxiety may have negative effects on intergroup relations (Gaertner and Dovidio 1986; Gudykunst 1995; Stephan and Stephan 1985). In this context, intergroup anxiety is not defined by discomfort surrounding the policy; rather, it represents apprehension surrounding future interactions with beneficiaries of the policy. However, there is reason to believe that intergroup anxiety may be importantly related to policy attitudes vis-à-vis the relationship between policy and beneficiary attitudes. This notion is derived from research showing that intergroup anxiety may be caused by negative attitudes toward and beliefs about the outgroup (Mackie, Devos, and Smith 2000), and research showing that people react (cognitively) to perceptions of threat by opposing social policies supporting the threatening outgroup (Durrheim et al. 2009; Sawires and Peacock 2000; Stephan, Ybarra, and Morrison 2009). For instance, individuals who feel threatened by same-sex marriage and oppose the policy may worry about being perceived as prejudiced during interaction with beneficiaries of same-sex marriage. Subsequent contact with policy beneficiaries under conditions of strong intergroup anxiety may lead to more negative evaluations of the outgroup (Stephan and Stephan 1985), promoting more negative attitudes toward the policy.

The remainder of this chapter is organized in the following way. Using the substantive example of same-sex marriage, the process of creating an initial item pool and selecting appropriate items via an item analysis is discussed, followed by an exploratory factor analysis on threat items to address their underlying factor structure. We subsequently show how a confirmatory factor analysis can be carried out to corroborate evidence gathered from an EFA. We end with a discussion about the structure of threat items in our example, and identify social policy contexts in which we would expect to find meaningful separation among realistic and symbolic threats.

4.   Development of ITT-Based Measures

Data was collected for 274 college students at a rural university in the Pacific Northwest. Eleven cases were deleted due to extensive missing data, with the final sample consisting of $n = 263$ participants ($M_{age} = 21$). Demographic characteristics are presented in Table 1.

Participants were recruited through a university student participation pool to fulfill research requirements or for extra credit. Students must have been at least 18 years old and enrolled in a psychology course to access the participation pool. The survey was administered in a quiet laboratory setting and took

Table 1. Demographic Characteristics of Study Respondents

		n	Percent
Gender	Female	206	75.5%
Ethnicity	White	139	51.1%
	Black	16	5.9%
	Hispanic/Latino	62	22.8%
	Multiracial	30	11.0%
	Asian/Asian-American	14	5.1%
	Native American	3	1.1%
	Other	8	2.9%
SES	Lower class	27	9.9%
	Lower-middle class	79	29%
	Middle class	110	40.4%
	Upper-middle class	53	19.5%
	Upper class	3	1.1%
Political ideology	Conservative	25	9.2%
	Middle of the road	83	30.6%
	Liberal	163	60.1%
Party ID	Democrat	135	52.5%
	Republican	18	7.0%
	Independent	50	19.5%
	Green	19	7.4%
	Other	35	13.6%
Sexual orientation[1]	Heterosexual	221	81.3%
	Gay/lesbian	21	7.7%
	Bisexual	30	11.0%
Relationship status	Single	187	68.8%
	Cohabitating	80	29.4%
	Married/widowed	4	1.5%
	Divorced/separated	1	0.4%
Registered Voter		165	60.4%
Religious or spiritual		148	54.4%
Regular church attendees[2]		99	44.4%

Note. [1]Data was analyzed excluding gay, lesbian, and bisexual respondents (i.e., potential outgroup members), and results did not appreciably differ. We decided to include all individuals regardless of sexual orientation to have the largest sample possible. [2]Regular church attendees defined as those who attended church at least once per month in the last year.

about 30 minutes to complete. It included three measures designed to assess perceptions of threat as they relate to same-sex marriage and its beneficiaries; namely, realistic threat, symbolic threat, and intergroup anxiety. All measures utilized a 10-point (0-9) scale. The realistic and symbolic threat scales were created for the present study because no measures addressed these threats in the extant literature. The process for selecting and creating realistic and symbolic threat items are delineated below.

4.1. Item Selection

Several of the realistic and symbolic threat items were adapted from a study on attitudes toward affirmative action (Renfro et al. 2006). We utilized media resources to construct the remaining threat items. Aside from being highly influential in affecting policy attitudes (Comstock and Paik 1991), news media may provide a rich source of arguments surrounding social policy, and therefore may prove an important place to search for item content in the development of threat measures. For example, an important source that we used to derive threat items came from California's Proposition 8 pamphlets and television commercials. Proposition 8, also known as the California Marriage Protection act, proposed an amendment to the state's constitution that would eliminate the rights of same-sex couples to marry. In the media coverage of Proposition 8, policy opponents focused on issues such as parental worry that children would be taught in school that homosexuality is normal, and that churches would be forced to perform same-sex marriages even if they did not agree with it. We would not have thought to include items such as these in our measures had we not focused on media resources in addition to the empirical literature.

4.1.1. Realistic threat

The realistic threat measure consists of eleven items, and examines perceptions of threat to heterosexuals' resources, political power, and welfare. Items were measured on a scale from (*strongly disagree*) to (*strongly agree*). A sample item is "Supporting same-sex marriage is a waste of taxpayer's money." Higher scores on this scale indicate greater perceptions of realistic threat.

4.1.2. Symbolic threat

The 11-item symbolic threat scale measures perceptions of threat to religious beliefs, morality, and the value system of heterosexuals. Items were measured on a scale from (*strongly disagree*) to (*strongly agree*) with statements such as "The legalization of same-sex marriage jeopardizes religious freedom" and "Same-sex marriage poses little or no threat to the cultural practices of the majority of Americans (reverse-scored)." Higher scores on this scale relate to greater perceptions of symbolic threat.

4.1.3. Intergroup anxiety

The intergroup anxiety measure was adapted from the Stephan and Stephan (1985) intergroup anxiety scale. Twelve items "anxious, apprehensive, comfortable, secure, worried, calm, confident, awkward, tense, carefree, nervous, and at ease" were measured on a scale ranging from (*not at all*) to (*extremely*) to assess participants' perceived anxiety when interacting with beneficiaries of same-sex marriage. This scale has shown good reliability in previous work examining attitudes toward beneficiaries of a social policy ($\alpha = .93$; Renfro et al. 2006). Higher scores indicate greater intergroup anxiety.

4.2. Analytic Techniques

4.2.1. Item analysis

An item analysis on the newly devised threat items consisted of entering the entire block of threat items for each measure into a reliability analysis, paying close attention to the corrected item-total correlations and the alpha if item deleted. The goal of this item analysis was not purely to maximize the alpha coefficient because internal consistency concerns should be balanced with broader concerns about construct validity. In other words, maximization of Cronbach's alpha is often at the expense of losing important information about the criterion (Raykov 2008), thus a qualitative analysis of item content should be used in combination with statistical procedures. To that end, low corrected item-total correlations (e.g., r's $< .20$) in conjunction with a qualitative analysis of item content determined whether an item was dropped from a scale. The purpose of the qualitative item analysis was to determine whether ambiguous wording was responsible for low corrected item-total correlations, and whether the items conveyed important content not otherwise captured by other items in the scale. Because realistic and symbolic threats tap distinct constructs (Bobo 1983), but have been strongly correlated in previous research (Renfro et al. 2006; Schweitzer et al. 2005), both exploratory and confirmatory factor analyses were employed to examine the factor structure of each threat variable.

4.2.2. Factor analysis

The use of confirmatory factor analysis (CFA) to address theoretical predictions of threat as they relate to ITT is, to our knowledge, the first work to utilize this methodology. Several studies that have incorporated realistic and symbolic threats utilized exploratory factor analysis (EFA) to address the factor structure of threat items, in which some studies found support for a different factor structure of realistic and symbolic threats (e.g., Durrheim et al. 2009), while others have not (e.g., Renfro et al. 2006). In EFA, a number of items that are presumed to measure a smaller number of constructs, abilities, or traits are analyzed with no a priori hypotheses about the underlying factor structure of those items. Decisions must be made about the number of factors to retain and the extraction method for factor rotation. This process is generally used to explore the interrelatedness of items in a test without any prior theory driving the process. With CFA, however, prior research and theory are used to confirm hypotheses with respect to the factor structure of test items. Because there is an established theoretical distinction between realistic and symbolic threats, studies employing these threats should utilize CFA to examine whether or not the data is adequately explained by the theoretical model.

Furthermore, CFA comprises the measurement component of structural equation modeling (SEM). Many studies utilizing ITT employ path analysis, in which composite variables (e.g., when individual items representing a construct are summed to create a composite measure of that construct) are assumed perfectly reliable measures of the underlying construct. SEM is a more powerful framework for testing these theoretical models because it utilizes latent variables, which are inferred from test items and do not assume perfect reliability in the latent constructs (i.e., they are measured with error). Thus, SEM, and its measurement component, CFA, is a more powerful framework than path analysis for testing the plausibility of causal relationships in correlational models, as long as the statistical assumptions for conducting SEM have been met.

Table 2. Means, Standard Deviations, Correlations, and α Coefficients among Study Variables

Variable	*M*	*SD*	Realistic threat	Symbolic threat	Intergroup anxiety
Realistic threat	19.13	14.21	α = .81	.81	.61
Symbolic threat	16.55	15.60		α = .88	.61
Intergroup anxiety	19.78	16.81			α = .91

Note. The possible range of values for realistic and symbolic threat was 0-81, and 0-108 for intergroup anxiety. All correlations significant at *p* < .05

4.3. Reliability of Measures

For realistic threat, an item analysis revealed two items that displayed low corrected item-total correlations (*r*'s of -.06 and .16): "Domestic partners and married people have the same rights under the law," and "States that allow weddings by same-sex couples will see an increase in tax revenue associated with wedding spending." These items were dropped from the final scale. Two additional items displayed moderately low corrected item-total correlations: "The government's focus on same-sex marriage issues has led it to ignore more pressing political issues and economic problems," and "If same-sex marriage was legalized, churches would be forced to perform same-sex marriages even if they did not agree with same-sex marriage (*r*'s of .25 and .26, respectively)." In this case, item content was deemed important and the two items were kept, resulting in a 9-item realistic threat measure (α = .81). For symbolic threat, two items were dropped from the scale after examining the corrected item-total correlations (*r*'s < .20) and determining that the item content was ambiguously worded and did not convey unique content. The dropped items are: "Same-sex marriage is a result of a change in values of the American population," and "Same-sex marriage is an attempt to legislate morality." The final 9-item scale evidenced good internal consistency reliability (α = .88). Lastly, the item analysis established that all items would be included in the intergroup anxiety scale (12 items; α = .91). Means, standard deviations, α coefficients, and correlations among study variables are displayed in Table 2 and threat items for the final scales are displayed in Table 3.

Table 3. Final Items Included in Realistic and Symbolic Threat Measures

Realistic threat	1. The government's focus on same-sex marriage issues has led it to ignore more pressing political issues and economic problems.
	2. Marital protections, such as social security and health care benefits, should be available to same-sex partners. (Reverse-scored)
	3. Parents should teach their children about marriage without public schools teaching their kids that gay marriage is okay.
	4. Supporting same-sex marriage is causing the U.S. to lose some of its political power.
	5. The purpose of marriage is to conceive children, therefore only a man and a woman should be married.
	6. If same-sex marriage was legalized, churches would be forced to perform same-sex marriages even if they did not agree with same-sex marriage.
	7. Recognition of same-sex marriage poses a threat to society because public schools will be forced to teach that homosexuality is normal.
	8. Same-sex marriage will lead to unnecessary financial burdens, such as social security and health care benefits.
	9. Supporting same-sex marriage is a waste of taxpayer's money.
Symbolic threat	1. Same-sex marriage poses little or no threat to the cultural practices of the majority of Americans. (Reverse-scored)
	2. Same-sex marriage undermines the meaning of the traditional family.
	3. The legalization of same-sex marriage jeopardizes religious freedom.
	4. Same-sex marriage violates the sanctity of marriage.
	5. Gay men and lesbians desire relationships similar in quality to heterosexuals. (Reverse-scored)
	6. The family will be strengthened by the recognition of same-sex marriages. (Reverse-scored)
	7. Same-sex marriage violates religious beliefs held by the American majority.
	8. Same-sex marriage damages society's moral standards.
	9. The values of gay men and lesbians regarding family are the same as those of heterosexuals.

Note. All items measured on a 10 point (0-9) scale from (*strongly disagree*) to (*strongly agree*). Higher scores indicate greater perceptions of threat.

4.4.   Do the Threat Measures Address Distinct Constructs?

Factors were expected to correlate, given that they share a common attitude object (same-sex marriage). As a result, an oblique rotation (Direct Oblimin) was utilized in the exploratory component/factor analysis of realistic threat, symbolic threat, and intergroup anxiety items. A common factor selection criteria is an Eigenvalue greater than one (Kaiser 1960). This approach determined that three factors would maximize the explained variance. However, examination of a scree plot determined that a two factor solution better fit the data and allowed for better interpretability of the factors. For the two factor solution, the unrotated Eigenvalues totaled 14.91, accounting for 49.7% of item variance. Evaluation of the structure matrix showed that realistic and symbolic threat items loaded onto one factor, labeled group threat (factor loadings ranged from .21 to .90), and intergroup anxiety items loaded onto a separate factor, labeled interpersonal threat (factor loadings ranged from .55 to .82; see Table 4). Parallel Analysis (Horn 1965) also indicated a two factor solution. Parallel analysis compares eigenvalues from an analysis to those generated by random data. Factors/components are retained if their eigenvalues exceed the respective eigenvalues estimated based on random data.

The confirmatory factor analysis was performed on threat items using the M*plus* modeling software (Muthén and Muthén 1998-2011). Other latent variable modeling software will handle simple structure CFA with similar ease, including commercial packages such as AMOS (Arbuckle 2006) and EQS (Bentler 1995), and free software such as the **lavaan** package (Rosseel in press) created for the R statistical software (R Development Core Team 2012). Conventional CFA posits that items loading onto a factor are strictly related to that factor, with no overlap among items. However, specifying such a simple structure with zero cross-loadings among threat items is not consistent with ITT, which posits that realistic and symbolic threats are strongly related. For example, a realistic threat item (e.g., supporting same-sex marriage is a waste of taxpayer's money) may have a symbolic component (e.g., same-sex marriage damages society's moral standards). Thus, model fit of a conventional CFA is not expected to be excellent–especially in this context, given the misfit of a three-factor model using exploratory procedures.

Goodness-of-fit was examined using the Comparative Fit Index (CFI), Tucker-Lewis Index (TLI), Root Mean Square Error of Approximation (RMSEA), and the chi-square statistic. Fit indices around the mid .90's, a RMSEA less than .05, and a non-significant chi-square statistic generally indicate mod-

Table 4. Rotated Factor Loadings and Communalities among Threat Items

	Group threat	Interpersonal threat	Communality
Damages society's moral standards[b]	**.90**	.56	.82
Violates sanctity of marriage[b]	**.83**	.53	.70
Loss of political power[a]	**.82**	.51	.68
Waste of taxpayer money[a]	**.82**	.51	.67
Undermines meaning of traditional family[b]	**.81**	.47	.65
Jeopardizes religious freedom[b]	**.80**	.47	.64
Public schools teach homosexuality is normal[a]	**.80**	.49	.63
Purpose of marriage is to conceive children[a]	**.76**	.47	.58
Financial burdens of same-sex marriage[a]	**.76**	.54	.60
Marital protections for policy beneficiaries[a]	**.73**	.55	.55
Threat to cultural practices[b]	**.72**	.38	.52
Same family values[b]	**.68**	.47	.48
Family strengthened by recognition of SSM[b]	**.65**	.40	.43
Public schools teach gay marriage[a]	**.51**	.30	.26
Violates religious beliefs[b]	**.49**	.24	.24
Similar relationship quality[b]	**.42**	.24	.18
Churches forced to perform same-sex marriages[a]	**.34**	.09	.13
Threat to political and economic power[a]	**.21**	.18	.05
Tense[c]	.46	**.82**	.67
Nervous[c]	.44	**.79**	.63
At ease[c]	.42	**.76**	.58
Calm[c]	.43	**.76**	.58
Anxious[c]	.56	**.75**	.60
Carefree[c]	.39	**.73**	.54
Awkward[c]	.45	**.72**	.52
Confident[c]	.40	**.72**	.51
Secure[c]	.38	**.65**	.43
Comfortable[c]	.35	**.60**	.36
Apprehensive[c]	.40	**.60**	.36
Worried[c]	.47	**.55**	.34
% explained	8.5	41.2	
Rotated Eigenvalue	9.4	10.9	
Rotated %	31.4	36.4	

Note. Principal components analysis with Direct Oblimin rotation. The non-orthogonal components explain 67.8% of item variance. SSM = same-sex marriage. [a]Realistic threat. [b]Symbolic threat. [c]Intergroup anxiety els that are plausible approximations of the data (Raykov and Marcoulides 2006). However, because calculation of the chi-square test statistic is influenced by sample size, statistical significance is expected with large samples. Model fit for the three factor CFA was satisfactory, $\chi^2(402, N = 263) = 814.67$, $p < .001$, CFI = .900, TLI = .891, RMSEA = .062, 90% RMSEA CI [.056, .069]. Factor loadings for the 9-item realistic threat measure ranged from .25 to .82. Loadings for the 9-item symbolic threat measure ranged from .35-.89, and loadings ranged from .53-.81 for the 12-item intergroup anxiety scale. The CFA revealed such a strong latent factor correlation between realistic and symbolic threats that the factors are nearly indistinguishable ($r = .98$), and both shared similar relationships with intergroup anxiety (r's of .69 and .66, respectively; see Figure 1).

5. Implications for Scale Development

In line with ITT, our example shows that social milieu is demonstrably important in deciding whether it is meaningful to distinguish between realistic and symbolic threats. Factor analytic results suggest that in the case of same-sex marriage, it is not meaningful to distinguish between the two measures of group threat. The remainder of this chapter focuses on plausible explanations for the substantial covariance among collective threat measures, identifying contexts in which we would expect greater separation among realistic and symbolic threats.

5.1. Collinearity of Threats

Multicollinearity (or collinearity) is an important statistical assumption of multiple regression analysis. It may be violated when two or more predictors in a regression model are correlated with one another at extremely high levels. Specifically, when variables in a regression model are correlated at $r \geq .70$, multicollinearity may be an issue (Tabachnick and Fidell 2001). With regression-based analyses, multicollinearity may affect precision of the estimates of individual predictors. This happens because the sampling variances of ordinary least squares (OLS) predictors increase with increasing collinearity, leading to larger confidence interval widths for each parameter and reduced statistical power to determine whether each variable measure something unique. Simply put, collinearity may turn important predictors into predictors that are not statistically significant.

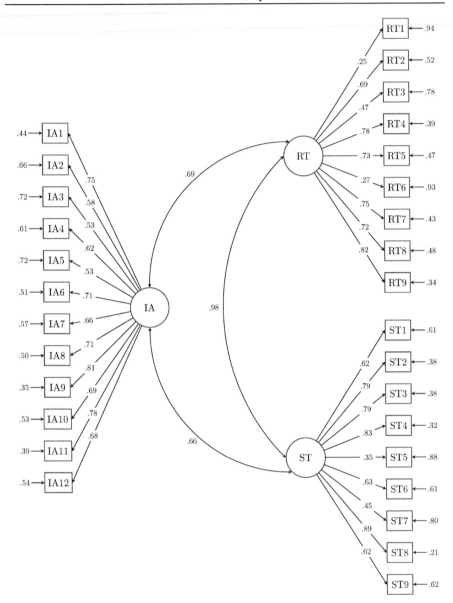

Figure 1. Confirmatory factor analysis diagram of threat items. IA = inter-group anxiety, RT = realistic threat, ST = symbolic threat.

Collinearity often suggests that a researcher included multiple measures of the same construct in a regression. This has historically been problematic among measures of realistic and symbolic threat in research on ITT. A meta-analytic assessment of intergroup threat found that realistic threats and symbolic threats share moderate to strong relationships (r's of .35 to .59), although it is common to see much stronger correlations among them (r's > .80).

In our example, the measured variables for realistic and symbolic threat was correlated at $r = .81$ (with an inflated latent factor correlation of $r = .98$), and both share nearly the same relationship with intergroup anxiety (r's of .61 for the measured variables; r's of .69 and .66, respectively, for the latent factors). Given that we did not find support for a different factor structure of realistic and symbolic threats, and that the covariance among our threat variables suggest that they measure something similar, it is likely that entering these variables as predictors in a regression (or akin, such as a structural equation model) would result in multicollinearity issues.

Because considerable overlap of realistic and symbolic threats is common in research on ITT, investigators have utilized novel approaches to demonstrate that they are conceptually distinct. For instance, in a study on affirmative action, investigators recruited a sample of students and had them rate the degree to which each item constituted a realistic threat versus a symbolic threat. For realistic threat, the authors asked "To what degree does the following item concern a loss of economic resources, political power, or threats to the physical well-being of the group" versus "To what degree does the following item concern issues or problems created by group differences in values, beliefs, customs, or norms?" for symbolic threat (Renfro et al., 2006, p. 47). This same manner of using definitional criteria to distinguish between realistic and symbolic threats has been used in other studies as well (e.g., Stephan et al. 2002).

We argue that, in ITT research, a lack of support for realistic and symbolic threat differences are not a criticism of the theory or, in many cases, the measures used in those studies. Rather, the social policy context may not warrant a distinction between realistic and symbolic threats, and ignoring this fact may lead to incorrect substantive conclusions regarding the impact of threats. In the following sections, we offer suggestions for why collinearity was present in our example on attitudes toward same-sex marriage, and offer suggestions for researchers facing similar data situations.

5.1.1. Floor or ceiling effects

Attitudes are often highly polarized and fiercely divided around social transformation policies–so much so that it may not be useful to distinguish between realistic and symbolic threats. In other words, people who oppose a policy may vehemently oppose it, and those who support it may do so invariably. In the case of same-sex marriage, this appears to be true: individuals with differing political views are highly divided on the issue; only 28% of conservatives and 78% of liberals endorse the policy (Gallup 2011), and our realistic and symbolic threat item distributions were generally positively skewed (leaning toward lower threat perceptions). This may reflect the fact that perceptions of threat surrounding same-sex marriage in the population may be non-normal, or it may have been partially a function of our sample, which contained few individuals with a conservative political ideology.

5.1.2. Realistic-symbolic threat dependencies

Although the constructs of realistic and symbolic threat are theoretically distinct, it is possible that in some contexts realistic threats are generated by people who hold strong symbolic threat perceptions (or vice versa). For instance, individuals may believe that same-sex marriage violates traditional values of gender and family (a symbolic threat) because at their core they do not think marriage can be between anyone other than a man and a woman (a realistic threat). Thus, in our example, a realistic-symbolic threat dependency may have been partially initiated by the primacy of symbolic threat, an issue that we turn to next.

5.1.3. Domination of symbolic threats

Among opponents of same-sex marriage, religion, traditional values, and morality are some of the most salient issues surrounding the same-sex marriage debate (Brewer and Wilcox 2005; Greene 2009; Olson, Cadge, and Harrison 2006), whereas proponents of the policy often appeal to principles of equality (Price, Nir, and Cappella 2005). In addition, news media coverage of same-sex marriage appears to follow a similar structure (Pan, Meng, and Zhou 2006). News media is highly influential in affecting the public's perceptions of and attitudes toward social policy, and this is especially true of same-sex marriage (Anderson, Fakhfakh, and Kondylis 1999; Comstock and Paik 1991). For example, a study that examined coverage of same-sex marriage in two popular media outlets, *The New York Times* and the *Chicago Tribune*, between the years of 2002 and 2004 found that among the two outlets, the *Chicago Tribune* focused on symbolic issues such as traditional family values and religion at a significantly higher rate than *The New York Times* (42% and 29%, respectively); whereas *The New York Times* focused on issues of equal rights at a significantly higher rate than the *Chicago Tribune* (Pan, Meng, and Zhou 2006). It is important to note that *The New York Times* openly supports same-sex marriage whereas the *Chicago Tribune* does not. This is not to say that coverage of same-sex marriage in the news media is a determining factor in public opinion about same-sex marriage, rather it is presented to underscore the importance of symbolic issues for those who do not openly endorse the policy.

5.1.4.   Realistic threat and resource competition

In the context of attitudes toward same-sex marriage, individuals may not separately endorse realistic and symbolic threat items because competition for resources is not an issue. When resource competition is present, a meaningful separation between realistic and symbolic threats is more likely. For instance, in a study on attitudes toward immigrants, researchers found that realistic and symbolic threat mediated the relationship between diversity beliefs and intentions to discriminate against immigrants when diversity was operationalized in general terms (i.e., as a value to society). However, in a subsequent study, the researchers operationalized diversity in terms of its benefits for worker productivity and, placed within this economic context, only realistic threat mediated the relationship between diversity beliefs and intentions to engage in discriminatory behavior (Kauff and Wagner 2012). Taken together, these findings suggest that realistic threat is more salient in contexts when resources are at stake.

Related to this idea of resource competition, it makes sense to distinguish between social transformation policies that are compensatory and those that provide preferential treatment (Durrheim et al. 2009). Compensatory programs enable disadvantaged groups to compete more successfully, whereas preferential treatment programs provide opportunities for historically disadvantaged groups at the expense of other groups (e.g., affirmative action programs based on quota systems; Tuch and Hughes 1996). By their very definitions, preferential treatment programs imply competition for resources whereas compensatory programs, such as same-sex marriage, do not. In a recent study examining attitudes toward compensatory and preferential treatment programs for Blacks in post-apartheid South Africa, researchers found that, for Whites, perceptions of realistic and symbolic threat were strong predictors of opposition to preferential treatment policies, but only symbolic threat was an important predictor of attitudes toward compensatory treatment programs (Durrheim et al. 2009). Additionally, in a study on attitudes toward affirmative action, researchers found evidence that resources played a differential role in policy support (Renfro et al. 2006). In that study, personal relevance of affirmative action was mediated by realistic but not symbolic threat. Thus, it is likely that opposition to affirmative action increases when individuals perceive that they will soon compete for jobs with its beneficiaries.

Conclusion

This chapter covered several important issues pertaining to the development of realistic and symbolic threat measures as they relate to social transformation policies. Using the example of attitudes toward same-sex marriage, we described the development of realistic and symbolic threat measures from the initial stage of item selection through the statistical analysis of item structure using factor analytic procedures. The addition of CFA for testing the plausibility of a different factor structure of realistic and symbolic threat measures is a new contribution for researchers in the threat arena. In contrast to exploratory factor analysis, CFA is employed when researchers have a priori hypotheses about the underlying factor structure of test items. Because realistic and symbolic threat are theoretically separate constructs, researchers analyzing these threats should incorporate CFA to confirm that the constructs are, in fact, distinct. In light of this recommendation, we hope that researchers will increasingly use CFA as a tool to aid decisions about whether there is sound justification to distinguish between realistic and symbolic threats. Although in some contexts it may not make sense to distinguish between them, we argue that both constructs should be included during data collection. During data analysis, if multicollinearity of realistic and symbolic threats is an issue, using the threat indicators from both measures to make up a composite (or latent) threat variable should be preferred to including a single threat measure, because more variance in policy attitudes is likely to be explained (and model fit is likely to improve; Stephan et al. 1998). Lastly, we hope that researchers measuring perceptions of threat toward social policy will think critically about the political, economic, geographic, and historical contexts in which social policy debates are nested, because such contexts may offer additional insight into whether a refined causal explanation of collective threat is necessary.

References

Aberson, C. L. and A. M. Gaffney (2009). "An integrated threat model of explicit and implicit attitudes". In: *European Journal of Social Psychology* 39, pp. 808–830. DOI: 10.1002/ejsp.582.

Anderson, P. B., A. Fakhfakh, and M. A. Kondylis (1999). "Attitudes toward the media's portrayals of gays and lesbians". In: *Electronic Journal of Human Sexuality* 2. URL: http://www.ejhs.org.

Arbuckle, J. L. (2006). *Amos (Version 7.0) [Computer Program]*. Chicago.

Bentler, P. M. (1995). *EQS (Version 5.7)*. Encino, CA.

Berrenberg, J. L. et al. (2002). "Prejudice toward people with cancer or AIDS: Applying the integrated threat model". In: *Journal of Applied Biobehavioral Research* 7, pp. 75–86. DOI: 10.1111/j.1751-9861.2002.tb000 78.x.

Biernat, M., T. K. Vescio, and S. A. Theno (1996). "Violating American values: A "value congruence" approach to understanding outgroup attitudes". In: *Journal of Experimental Social Psychology* 32, pp. 387–410. DOI: 10.1006/jesp.1996.0018.

Bizman, A. and Y. Yinon (2001). "Intergroup and interpersonal threats as determinants of prejudice: The moderating role of in-group identification". In: *Basic and Applied social Psychology* 23, pp. 191–196. DOI: 10.1207/153248301750433669.

Bobo, L. (1983). "Whites' opposition to busing: Symbolic racism or realistic group conflict?" In: *Journal of Personality and Social Psychology* 45, pp. 1196–1210. DOI: 10.1037/0022-3514.45.6.1196.

Bobo, L. and V. L. Hutchings (1996). "Perceptions of Racial Group Competition: Extending Blumer's Theory of Group Position to a Multiracial Social Context". In: *American Sociological Review* 61, pp. 951–972. DOI: doi:10.2307/2096302.

Bobo, L. and M. Tuan (2006). *Prejudice in politics: Group position, public opinion, and the Wisconsin treaty rights dispute*. Cambridge: Harvard University Press.

Brewer, P. R. and C. Wilcox (2005). "The polls-trends: Same-sex marriage and civil unions". In: *Public Opinion Quarterly* 69, pp. 599–616. DOI: 10.1093/poq/nfi052.

Charles-Toussaint, G. C. and H. M. Crowson (2010). "Prejudice against International Students: The Role of Threat Perceptions and Authoritarian Dispositions in U.S. Students". In: *The Journal of Psychology: Interdisciplinary and Applied* 144, pp. 413–428. DOI: 10.1080/00223980.2010.496643.

Comstock, G. and H. Paik (1991). *Television and the American child.* New York: Academic Press.

Corenblum, B. and W. G. Stephan (2001). "White fears and Native apprehensions: An integrated threat theory approach to intergroup attitudes". In: *Canadian Journal of Behavioural Science* 33.4, pp. 251–268.

Crocker, J., B. Major, and C. Steele (1998). "Social stigma". In: *The handbook of social psychology, Vols. 1 and 2 (4th ed.)* Ed. by D. T. Gilbert, S. T. Fiske, and G. Lindzey. New York, NY: McGraw-Hill, pp. 504–553.

Curseu, P. L., R. Stoop, and R. Schalk (2007). "Prejudice toward immigrant workers among Dutch employees: Integrated threat theory revisited". In: *European Journal of Social Psychology* 37, pp. 125–140. DOI: 10.1002/ejsp.331.

Durrheim, K. et al. (2009). "Predicting support for racial transformation policies: Intergroup threat, racial prejudice, sense of group entitlement and strength of identification". In: *European Journal of Social Psychology* 39, pp. 1–25. DOI: 10.1002/ejsp.723.

Esses, V. M., G. Haddock, and M. P. Zanna (1993). "Values, stereotypes, and emotions as determinants of intergroup attitudes". In: *Affect, cognition, and stereotyping: Interactive processes in group perception.* Ed. by D. M. Mackie and D. L. Hamilton. San Diego, CA: Academic Press, pp. 137–166.

Gaertner, S. L. and J. F. Dovidio (1986). "The aversive form of racism". In: *Prejudice, discrimination, and racism.* Ed. by J. F. Dovidio and S. L. Gaertner. New York, NY: Greenwood Publishing Group, pp. 61–89.

Gallup (May 2011). *For first time, majority of Americans favor legal gay marriage.* URL: http://www.gallup.com/poll/147662/first-time-majority-americans-favor-legal-gay-marriage.aspx.

González, K. V. et al. (2008). "Prejudice towards Muslims in the Netherlands: Testing integrated threat theory". In: *British Journal of Social Psychology* 47, pp. 667–685. DOI: 10.1348/014466608X284443.

Greene, B. (2009). "The use and abuse of religious beliefs in dividing and conquering between socially marginalized groups: The same-sex marriage debate". In: *American Psychologist* 64, pp. 698–709. DOI: 10.1037/000 3-066X.64.8.698.

Gudykunst, W. D. (1995). "Anxiety/uncertainty management (AUM) theory: Current status". In: *Intercultural communication theory*. Ed. by R. Wiseman. Thousand Oaks, CA, US: Sage Publications, Inc, pp. 8–58.

Haddock, G., M. P. Zanna, and V. M. Esses (2008). "Assessing the structure of prejudicial attitudes: The case of attitudes toward homosexuals". In: *Journal of Personality and Social Psychology* 65, pp. 1105–1118. DOI: 10.1037/0022-3514.65.6.1105.

Horn, J. L. (1965). "A rationale and test for the number of factors in factor analysis". In: *Psychometrika* 32, pp. 179–185. DOI: 10.1007/BF0228944 7.

Huddy, L. and D. O. Sears (2008). "Opposition to bilingual education: Prejudice or the defense of realistic interests?" In: *Social Psychology Quarterly* 58, pp. 133–143. DOI: 10.2307/2787151.

Johnson, D., D. J. Terry, and W. R. Louis (2008). "Perceptions of the intergroup structure and anti-Asian prejudice among white Australians". In: *Group Processes & Intergroup Relations* 8, pp. 53–71. DOI: 10.1177/1368430205048616.

Kaiser, H. F. (1960). "The application of electronic computers to factor analysis". In: *Educational and Psychological Measurement* 20, pp. 141–151. DOI: 10.1177/001316446002000116.

Kamans, E. et al. (2010). "How groups contest depends on group power and the likelihood that power determines victory and defeat". In: *Group Processes & Intergroup Relations* 13, pp. 715–724. DOI: 10.1177/13684302 10375252.

Kauff, M. and U. Wagner (2012). "Valuable Therefore not Threatening: The Influence of Diversity Beliefs on Discrimination Against Immigrants". In: *Social Psychological and Personality Science* 0, pp. 1–8. DOI: 10.1177/1948550611435942.

Kinder, D. R. and D. O. Sears (1981). "Prejudice and politics: Symbolic racism versus racial threats to the good life". In: *Journal of Personality and Social Psychology* 40, pp. 414–431. DOI: 10.1037/0022-3514.40.3.414.

Kluegel, J. R. and E. R. Smith (1983). "Affirmative action attitudes: Effects of self-interest, race affect, and stratification beliefs on Whites' views". In: *Social Forces* 61, pp. 797–824. DOI: 10.2307/2578135.

Leong, C. H. and C. Ward (2011). "Intergroup Perceptions and Attitudes toward Immigrants in a Culturally Plural Society". In: *Applied Psychology:*

An International Review 60, 46âĂŞ65. DOI: 10.1111/j.1464-0597.20 10.00426.x.

LeVine, R. A. and D. T. Campbell (1972). *Ethnocentrism: Theories of conflict, ethnic attitudes, and group behavior.* Oxford, England: John Wiley & Sons.

Mackie, D. M., T. Devos, and E. R. Smith (2000). "Intergroup emotions: Explaining offensive action tendencies in an intergroup context". In: *Journal of Personality and Social Psychology* 79, pp. 602–616. DOI: 10.1037/0022-3514.79.4.602.

Matera, C., C. Stefanile, and R. Brown (2011). "The role of immigrant acculturation preferences and generational status in determining majority intergroup attitudes". In: *Journal of Experimental Social Psychology* 47, pp. 776–785. DOI: 10.1016/j.jesp.2011.03.007.

McConahay, J. B. (1983). "Modern racism and modern discrimination: The effects of race, racial attitudes, and context on simulated hiring decisions". In: *Personality and Social Psychology Bulletin* 9, pp. 551–558. DOI: 10.1 177/0146167283094004.

McConahay, J. B. and J. C. Hough (1976). "Symbolic racism". In: *Journal of Social Issues* 32, pp. 23–45. DOI: 10.1111/j.1540-4560.1976.tb0249 3.x.

Muthén, L. K. and B. Muthén (1998-2011). *Mplus (Version 6.12).* Los Angeles.

Olson, L. R., W. Cadge, and J. T. Harrison (2006). "Religion and public opinion about same-sex marriage". In: *Social Science Quarterly* 87, pp. 340–360. DOI: 10.1111/j.1540-6237.2006.00384.x.

Osborne, D., P G. Davies, and A. Duran (2008). "The integrated threat theory and politics: Explaining attitudes toward political parties". In: *Personality and Social Psychology Research.* Ed. by B. P. Reimann. New York: Nova Science Publishers, Inc, pp. 61–74.

Pan, P. L., J. Meng, and S. Zhou (2006). "Morality or equality? Ideological framing in news coverage of gay marriage legitimization". In: *The Social Science Journal* 47, pp. 630–645. DOI: 10.1016/j.soscij.2010.02.00 2.

Patterson, C. J. (2006). "Children of lesbian and gay parents: Psychology, law, and policy". In: *American Psychologist* 64, pp. 727–736. DOI: 10.1037/ 0003-066X.64.8.727.

Pettigrew, T. F., U. Wagner, and O. Christ (2010). "Population Ratios and Prejudice: Modelling Both Contact and Threat Effects". In: *Journal of Ethnic and Migration Studies* 36, pp. 635–650. DOI: 10.1080/13691830903516 034.

Price, V., L. Nir, and J. N. Cappella (2005). "Framing public discussion of gay civil unions". In: *Public Opinion Quarterly* 69, pp. 179–212. DOI: 10.1093/poq/nfi014.

R Development Core Team (2012). *R: A Language and Environment for Statistical Computing*. ISBN 3-900051-07-0. R Foundation for Statistical Computing. Vienna, Austria. URL: http://www.R-project.org.

Raykov, T. (2008). "Alpha if Item Deleted: A Note on Criterion Validity Loss in Scale Revision if Maximising Coefficient Alpha". In: *British Journal of Mathematical and Statistical Psychology* 61, pp. 275–285. DOI: 10.134 8/000711007X188520.

Raykov, T. and G. A. Marcoulides (2006). *A First Course in Structural Equation Modeling (2nd ed.)*. Mahwah, New Jersey: Lawrence Erlbaum Associates, Inc.

Renfro, C. L et al. (2006). "The role of threat in attitudes toward affirmative action and its beneficiaries". In: *Journal of Applied Social Psychology* 36, pp. 41–74. DOI: 10.1111/j.0021-9029.2006.00003.x.

Richeson, J. A. and S. Trawalter (2005). "Why do interracial interactions impair executive function? A resource depletion account". In: *Journal of Personality and Social Psychology* 88, pp. 934–947. DOI: 10.1037/0022-3514.88.6.934.

Riek, B. M., E. W. Mania, and S. L. Gaertner (2006). "Intergroup threat and outgroup attitudes: A meta-analytic review". In: *Personality and Social Psychology Review* 10, pp. 336–353. DOI: 10.1207/s15327957pspr100 4_4.

Riek, B. M. et al. (2010). "Does a common ingroup identity reduce intergroup threat?" In: *Group Processes & Intergroup Relations* 13, pp. 403–423. DOI: 10.1177/1368430209346701.

Rohmann, A., A. Florack, and U. Piontkowski (2006). "The role of discordant acculturation attitudes in perceived threat: An analysis of host and immigrant attitudes in Germany". In: *International Journal of Intercultural Relations* 30, pp. 683–702. DOI: 10.1016/j.ijintrel.2006.06.006.

Rosseel, Y. (in press). "lavaan: An R Package For Structural Equation Modeling". In: *Journal of Statistical Software*.

Sawires, J. N. and M. J. Peacock (2000). "Symbolic racism and voting behavior on Proposition 209". In: *Journal of Applied Social Psychology* 30, pp. 2092–2099. DOI: 10.1111/j.1559-1816.2000.tb02426.x.

Schweitzer, R. et al. (2005). "Attitudes towards Refugees: The Dark Side of Prejudice in Australia". In: *Australian Journal of Psychology* 57, pp. 170–179. DOI: 10.1080/00049530500125199.

Sears, D. O. (1988). "Eliminating racism: Profiles in controversy". In: *Perspectives in social psychology*. Ed. by P. A. Katz and D. A. Taylor. New York, NY: Plenum Press, pp. 53–84.

Sears, D. O. and H. M. Allen (1984). "The trajectory of local desegregation controversies and Whites' opposition to busing". In: *Groups in contact: The psychology of desegregation*. Ed. by N. Miller and M. B. Brewer. New York: Academic Press, pp. 123–151.

Sears, D. O. and J. Citrin (1985). *Tax revolt: Something for nothing in California*. Cambridge, MA: Harvard University Press.

Sears, D. O. and L. Huddy (1993). "The trajectory of local desegregation controversies and Whites' opposition to busing". In: *Conflict between people and peoples*. Ed. by S. Worchel and J. A. Simpson. Chicago: Nelson-Hall, pp. 145–169.

Sears, D. O. and D. R. Kinder (1993). "Racial tensions and voting in Los Angeles". In: *Los Angeles: Viability and prospects for metropolitan leadership*. Ed. by W. Z. Hersch. New York: Praeger, pp. 51–88.

Semyonov, M. et al. (2004). "Population size, perceived threat, and exclusion: A multiple-indicators analysis of attitudes toward foreigners in Germany". In: *Social Science Research* 33, pp. 681–701. DOI: 10.1016/j.ssresearch.2003.11.003.

Sherif, M. (1966). *Group conflict and cooperation*. London: Routledge and Kegan Paul.

Sibley, C. J. and J. H. Liu (2004). "Attitudes towards biculturalism in New Zealand: Social dominance and Pakeha attitudes towards the general principles and resource-specific aspects of bicultural policy". In: *New Zealand Journal of Psychology* 33.2, pp. 88–99.

Sniderman, P. M. and P. E. Tetlock (1986). "Reflections on American racism". In: *Journal of Social Issues* 42, pp. 173–187. DOI: 10.1111/j.1540-4560.1986.tb00231.x.

Stephan, C. W. et al. (2000). "Women's attitudes toward men: An integrated threat theory approach". In: *Psychology of Women Quarterly* 24, pp. 63–73. DOI: 10.1111/j.1471-6402.2000.tb01022.x.

Stephan, W. G., R. Diaz-Loving, and A. Duran (2000). "Integrated threat theory and intercultural attitudes: Mexico and the United States". In: *Journal of Cross-Cultural Psychology* 31, pp. 240–249. DOI: 10.1177/00220221 00031002006.

Stephan, W. G. and C. W. Stephan (1985). "Intergroup anxiety". In: *Journal of Social Issues* 41, pp. 157–175. DOI: 10.1111/j.1540-4560.1985.tb 01134.x.

Stephan, W. G. and C. W. Stephan (2000). "An integrated threat theory of prejudice". In: *Reducing prejudice and discrimination.* Ed. by S. Oskamp. Mahwah, NJ: Lawrence Erlbaum, pp. 23–45.

Stephan, W. G., O. Ybarra, and G. Bachman (1999). "Prejudice Toward Immigrants". In: *Journal of Applied Social Psychology* 29, pp. 2221–2237. DOI: 10.1111/j.1559-1816.1999.tb00107.x.

Stephan, W. G., O. Ybarra, and K. R. Morrison (2009). "Intergroup threat theory". In: *Handbook of prejudice, stereotyping, and discrimination.* Ed. by T. D. Nelson. New York, NY: Psychology Press, pp. 43–59.

Stephan, W. G. et al. (1998). "Prejudice Toward Immigrants to Spain and Isreal: An integrated threat theory analysis". In: *Journal of Cross-Cultural Psychology* 29, pp. 559–576. DOI: 10.1177/0022022198294004.

Stephan, W. G. et al. (2002). "The role of threats in the racial attitudes of Blacks and Whites". In: *Personality and Social Psychology Bulletin* 28, pp. 1242–1254. DOI: 10.1177/01461672022812009.

Stephan, W. G. et al. (2005). "The effects of feeling threatened on attitudes toward immigrants". In: *International Journal of Intercultural Relations* 29, pp. 1–19. DOI: 10.1016/j.ijintrel.2005.04.011.

Stivers, A. and A. Valls (2007). "Same-sex marriage and the regulation of language". In: *Politics, Philosophy, & Economics* 6, pp. 237–253. DOI: 10.1177/1470594X07077275.

Tabachnick, T. B. and L. S. Fidell (2001). *Using Multivariate Statistics.* Boston, MA: Allyn and Bacon.

Tausch, N., M. Hewstone, and R. Roy (2009). "The relationships between contact, status, and prejudice: An integrated threat theory analysis of Hindu-Muslim relations in India". In: *Journal of Community and Applied Social Psychology* 19, pp. 83–94. DOI: 10.1002/casp.984.

Tetlock, P. E. (2007). "Psychology and politics: The challenges of integrating levels of analysis in social science". In: *Social psychology: Handbook of basic principles (2nd ed.)* Ed. by A. W. Kruglanski and T. E. Higgins. New York, NY: Guilford Press, pp. 888–912.

Trawalter, S., J. A. Richeson, and J. N. Shelton (2009). "Predicting behavior during interracial interactions: A stress and coping approach".

In: *Personality and Social Psychology Review* 13, pp. 243–268. DOI: 10.1177/1088868309345850.

Tuch, S. A. and M. Hughes (1996). "Whites' racial policy attitudes". In: *Social Science Quarterly* 77.4, pp. 723–745.

INDEX

G

H

I

S

T

U

V